cruise hosting

Brooke Shannon Bravos, CTP

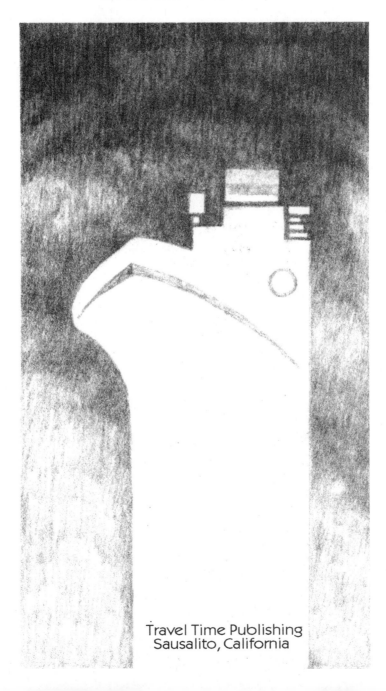

Travel Time Publishing
Sausalito, California

Cruise Hosting
Brooke Shannon Bravos, CTP
Copyright © 1992 Travel Time Publishing

Travel Time Publishing
P.O. Box 233, Sausalito, CA 94966 USA
(415) 331-1808

Trademarks

Notice of Liability

Library of Congress Cataloging 91-91400 CIP

ISBN 0-9630614-9-6 $19.95 U.S.

10 9 8 7 6 5 4 3 2 1

Printed in the United States of America
by Malloy Lithographing, Inc., Ann Arbor, Michigan

This book is dedicated to my mother, with love.

Acknowledgments

I deeply appreciate the assistance given me by the many individuals who played a part in the development of *Cruise Hosting*. In particular, I thank the International Tour Management Institute (ITMI) for its training and support, Diana Persons and Dan Ilves at Olson Travelworld for cruise opportunities they have given me for the past seven years, and the numerous fellow cruise hosts and ITMI graduates who shared their ideas and experiences with me.

A special thanks to Kathleen Bennett, former passenger services representative for Royal Cruise Lines, who provided a cruise line point of view. I am also indebted to Cruise Lines International Association (CLIA) for its kind permission to reprint materials from its cruise manual. To all the cruise lines and airlines who granted me permission to use their documents as illustrations — Royal Cruise Line, Princess Cruise Line, Holland America Westours, Dolphin Cruise Line, and United Airlines — I also extend my thanks.

I am grateful to Lynn and Joe Duval (The Broadcaster) for many hours of computer scanning and for their unending support; to Linda Riquier (L & M Marketing) for her manuscript review; Sue Arnold (Working With Words) for getting the first draft structured and formatted, and Laurel Cook (A Way with Words) for editing the book through its subsequent drafts and for being there for me when the going got rough.

Fisher-Dizick Design and Publishing (Corte Madera, California) deserves much credit for its consummate skill in book design and production. Phillip Dizick was responsible for the cover design and finished art as well as page layout and paste-up. Deborah Fisher provided overall production management; interior page layout, design and formatting; and PageMaker consultation. And, most importantly, they both gave me their continuing support and friendship.

Kathee Speranza created the wonderful cartoons and illustrations that appear throughout the book as well as the ship design used on the cover.

I thank my husband for his expert advice and understanding throughout the course of this project that kept me at the computer all hours of the day and night.

Finally, a special thanks goes to my mother and father who always told me I could do anything I wanted as long as I was willing to work hard.

Contents

Part I Getting Started

Chapter 1

Using Available Resources 19

Chapter 2

Assembling Documents 31

Chapter 3

Developing Your Paperwork 41

Chapter 4

Preparing Handouts 55

Part II Ship Ahoy

Appendix

List of Examples

Preface

Over the past 20 years the cruise industry has seen tremendous growth. It has soared from 500,000 passengers in 1970 to over three million in 1990. By the year 2,000, the industry expects to see ten million passengers cruising annually.

What was once simply a mode of transportation (however luxurious) to take passengers from point A to point B is now viewed as a floating resort/spa. A vacation can start from and return to the same port or point of origin or the cruise can be combined with pre- and post-cruise tours to exotic countries and cities.

What has created this shift? For one thing, attitudes about taking cruises are changing; the age group availing itself of this kind of vacation is opening up to younger people and to singles. There is a shift to shorter three to seven-day cruises, and many more group tours are being booked at attractive discount rates.

Historically, cruise lines have valued their repeat passengers — the ones who have been cruising with them for years. Today many cruise lines are beginning to recognize the huge untapped market of first-time cruisers. To zero in on this lucrative market, cruise lines are now using newer, bigger and more elegant ships for the shorter itineraries that seem to appeal to this population. Today's ships vary from smaller, deluxe adventure cruise ships to larger "floating resorts" capable of accommodating 2,400 or more passengers. To handle the present and projected volume, 12 new ships were launched in 1992 and another 9 are scheduled to be launched by the end of 1994. This increase in capacity alone promises to have a great impact on the industry.

In the competition for clients, some cruise lines have had to cut back on costs, often in the area of ship's personnel. With fewer crew members, it's obvious that overall service will be affected. As a potential cruise host, however, you can turn the cruise line's "crisis" into a terrific opportunity. According to a vice president of a major cruise line, only ten percent of the cruise hosts who go on board the ships today are considered professionals.

Cruise Hosting was written: (1) for women and men who are not familiar with but who are interested in cruise hosting as a profession, (2) to provide ideas for cruise hosts who know the ropes but are interested in raising the level of knowledge they now possess and upgrading the service they now provide, (3) to inform group leaders and travel agencies about ways to work more efficiently with the on-board staff and to give them tips, shortcuts and ideas to help create a more enjoyable cruise experience for their clients and (4) for tour operators to help them become aware of what cruise hosts need to do their job as professionals.

As a training manual, the book is filled with suggestions — the what to do and the how to do it (as well as the what *not* to do.) The information you will receive from reading this book may, at times, seem overwhelming as there is much to learn and do as a professional cruise host. The rewards of the profession, however, are well worth it: lasting friendships, the possibility of seeing the world, the satisfaction of contributing to others, and much more. So read on, and welcome to the world of professional cruise hosting!

A New Career

Professional cruise hosting is a new and exciting career that has evolved with the growing popularity of vacation cruising. A professional cruise host contracts with a tour operator or travel agency to take groups on board cruise ships and provide them with a myriad of services for the duration of the cruise. Knowledge and training are necessary to perform competently as a professional.

Although it is a profession that demands special skills — as you will see in the pages to follow — the good news is that most of those skills can be acquired. Your age and gender are not as important as an upbeat attitude, good health and physical stamina. And your present occupation or college degree is not the key. The key is that you:

- ⚓ Enjoy traveling
- ⚓ Like people
- ⚓ Are a good listener
- ⚓ Use common sense to solve problems
- ⚓ Stay calm in emergencies
- ⚓ Have a creative flair
- ⚓ Love to host parties.

To be successful as a cruise host, you will need to learn how to work with the ship's staff and what services you can and cannot promise your passengers.

A cruise host usually works as an independent contractor, which means you are not considered an employee and can often work for more than one tour operator.

Remuneration

Depending on the company you work for, cruise hosts are paid (at this time of writing) approximately $50 to $70 a day base pay in addition to airfare, meals and accommodations throughout the cruise. Some companies will provide you free shore excursions but that is an extra and not to be expected. Most tour operators will also pay you for what are called "positioning days," i.e., any pre-cruise travel days required to get you to your point of embarkation. In this case, you should be paid for all airfare, hotel, meals and local transportation expenses in addition to your daily base rate. Pre- and post-cruise tour days are also provided if the company contracted with you to accompany those tours. Some companies also provide a laundry allowance while you are on tour — usually under $3 a day.

Finally, you can expect to receive gratuities from the passengers in your group. The suggested amount depends on (1) your tour operator's tipping policy, (2) whether or not the policy has been properly conveyed to the clients, (3) the size of the group, and (4) most important, how you perform on the cruise. Often cruise hosts are regarded as being in the same category as the ship's social staff. The social staff does not accept gratuities from passengers.

When you take into consideration that all expenses are taken care of and that the position comes with many extras, this compensation is an excellent reward for such an exciting job.

Who Hires You

Cruise hosts are hired directly by tour operators — the people who package tours — or through travel agencies who sell to the public. They are never hired directly through the cruise line. In this handbook, I refer only to *tour operators* but travel agencies are included in this nomenclature.

Here's how it works. Whenever a tour operator has booked approximately 15 passengers on a particular cruise, the booking qualifies as a "group." The tour operator receives a complimentary berth (not a cabin) from the cruise line, which means that someone is permitted to travel free — usually the person serving as cruise host or group leader. Because cruise hosting has not yet become a widely acknowledged profession in its own right, many times the cruise host will be: (1) the tour operator or travel agent who put the group together and wants to go along for a free vacation, (2) the tour operator's secretary who has done a good job all year and is being rewarded with a trip, or (3) a group leader of an "affinity groups" (a family group, church, club, etc.) who wants a free trip, professional recognition or both. However, because they are not trained professionals, they typically do little more than play social host at a pre-arranged cocktail party. They perform very few of the many duties we will be discussing in the pages that follow.

Because you are hired by the tour operator, you become, in effect, that company's business agent. In this capacity, you must make sure that the company gets everything it contracted for and paid the cruise line for on behalf of the cruise passengers, such as:

- ⚓ Cabin assignments in specific categories
- ⚓ Prepaid shore excursions
- ⚓ On-board ship credits (usually $25 to $150 per passenger)
- ⚓ Extra amenities, such as flowers or champagne
- ⚓ Complimentary cocktail parties
- ⚓ Prepaid staff gratuities (maitre d', cabin steward, waiters)

A cruise host also acts as business agent for the *clients*, making sure they are getting everything they paid for in their vacation package.

As the profession of cruise hosting developes it will have a tremendous impact on tour companies in the future. People pay a great deal of money for a cruise. Not only do they want and expect special attention, they believe everything should be absolutely perfect — just like on TV commercials. Companies that fail to provide a professional cruise host to accompany their groups might be missing the boat (no pun intended)!

When a professional cruise host accompanies a group on board a cruise ship, everyone wins. The passengers win because the special attention they get will usually assure them a more pleasurable cruise. The tour operator wins because the clients associate their good time with that company. Because they feel well taken care of, these clients will give that tour operator repeat business. The cruise line wins because any time passengers are happy and sharing their good time with others, the atmosphere on the whole ship is enlivened. And the cruise host wins because contented customers are a source of great personal satisfaction as well as financial reward in the form of gratuities and repeat clientele.

Your Responsibilities

As a professional cruise host you should be available at all times while on board the ship. You will provide an extra level of service to your clients, arranging activities and providing valuable information about ports, disembarkation procedures and customs regulations. Besides completing various reports for your tour operator, as described in chapter 14, you also assist the ship's staff in solving your clients' problems, and act as social hosts (for your clients) on ship and on shore excursions. You may also be required to make arrangements in case of emergency. Above all, you are there to make sure your clients have the best possible cruise experience.

Also as cruise host you will accompany your group from the starting point of the tour, or from the time everyone has boarded the ship, until the group disembarks the ship or reaches its final destination.

You may be wondering why independent cruise hosts are needed. Doesn't the ship's staff do everything? The fact is that the staff on a cruise ship has its hands full. They work many jobs and many long hours. If you can help with your own group's problems and needs, it takes a great burden off the ship's staff. In addition, ship's personnel find it much easier to deal with one person — the cruise host — than 50 to 100 individual passengers. Because it is critical that you work well with the ship's staff, the ins and outs of those relationships are stressed repeatedly throughout the book.

So, if you have a knack for connecting with people and making them feel welcome, and think you would enjoy the cruise industry, read on. This book will give you the knowledge and tools you need to be a professional cruise host. If you are someone who is already working as a cruise host, the information packed into this guide book will help you sharpen your skills and take a fresh look at your profession.

part I

getting started

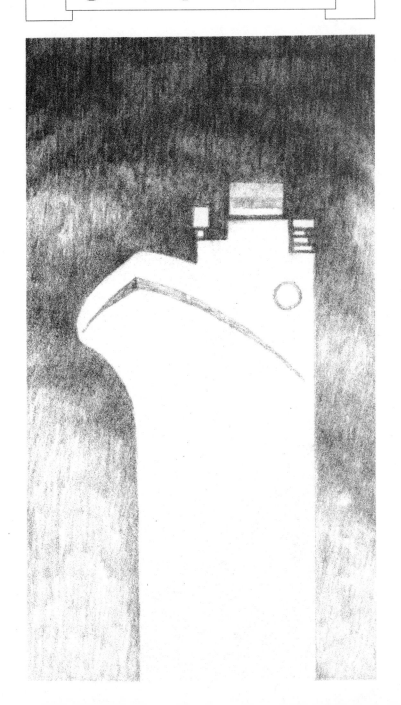

Chapter 1

Using Available Resources

You have been assigned a cruise, and you're excited (perhaps nervous), and rarin' to go. What now?

The first thing you will want to do is research the destination(s) to which you and your group are headed. Regardless of whether you have been there before, as a professional cruise host, you need to be ready with information and able to anticipate your passengers' questions. Start by gathering the best maps possible and highlighting the areas you will visit. This will give you a "mental picture" of where you will be traveling. Next, read over the cruise itinerary to see what is included. Highlight all tourist attractions en route. Look through books with photographs to get a visual picture of the area. The more research you do the more excited you will be about your trip, and the more valuable you will be to your tour clients. Also, research the cruise line on which you will be sailing. Clients will ask such questions as: How big is the ship? What country is she registered in? What nationality is the crew? How many passengers and crew members are on board? And during the cruise, your clients will come to you for details about the ship, shore excursions and ports of call.

Fortunately, there are a variety of resources available to you for your research. This chapter contains many you can use and describes the type of information each one provides. This information will be invaluable, especially when the destination of the cruise is new to you. As you travel you will want to collect materials for your own personal files. On subsequent cruises you'll be glad you did. You can take what you learn and work it into your port letters and briefing notes (see chapter 4.)

Organizations
Tourist Bureaus and Foreign Government Tourist Offices

Tourist bureaus and foreign government tourist offices will provide you with information and maps of the countries they represent. Offices are located in major cities, some agencies having offices only in New York. When calling or writing for information, state that you are a cruise host and give the name of the tour operator you work for. This adds credibility to your request.

Be sure to request the special detailed information available only to travel agents and travel writers. Also request country and city maps, including walking tours (if available). Some offices will provide free videos of the region or will rent them for a nominal fee. Videos are a wounderful way to get a feel for the area.

Tourist bureaus love to provide you with information to help promote their destinations. They will send you information on restaurants, shopping, cultural events, sightseeing attractions, transportation and survival tips. It often takes a few weeks to receive this material, so be sure to make your requests well in advance.

The appendix contains a list of tourist bureaus in alphabetical order by country. Each office was asked for the location of their bureaus in the major cities of New York, Los Angeles, San Francisco and Chicago, as well as in the states of Florida, Texas and Georgia.

Public Library

Check out books and magazines (such as *National Geographic*) on the countries you will visit. Look in the children's section, also, where you will find books with simple descriptions and explanations that are easy to understand and to the point. Again, videos are often available.

International Carriers and National Airlines

Call the regional sales office for the international airline you are using or the national airlines of the country for which you need information. Some airlines will ask you to write a formal letter of request on company stationery, and to include a business card. Others will ask you to come into the district sales office with your business card. It is strongly suggested that before you make any requests on company stationary you check with your tour operator.

Cruise Lines International Association Manual (CLIA)

CLIA is an organization whose primary mission is to support and train travel agents who sell and market cruises. Affiliate agencies receive discounts on familiarization cruises, videos on sales training and cruise destinations and customized travel bags (with their logo).

Only travel agencies are eligible to join CLIA. If you are a member, the annual cruise manual is free. Non-members can purchase it for $75. For most cruise hosts $75 is a big investment, but it is well worth the price. It is the first book I turn to when assigned a cruise.

The annually revised cruise manual includes all the newest ships to be launched that year and contains almost 600 pages of valuable information about the cruise lines that are members of the association. Here you will find excellent copies of the ships' diagrams and a full page of information about each ship, including accommodations, public room capacities (for planning briefings and parties) and other facilities. It contains sample menus, samples of the ship's daily newspaper as well as telephone numbers and addresses for each member cruise line's sales office.

In the back of the manual are 36 country maps showing various ports and dock locations. Information includes how long it takes to get from the port to the airport, available transportation to the airport and parking facilities at the dock. (See appendix for sample pages and glossary from the CLIA manual.)

CLIA also has a cruise video library that highlights member ships, showing their amenities and entertainments and giving overviews of cruising. For example, Royal Viking's "Grand Circle Pacific" previews its 100-day cruise. The South America and Rio tape includes the ports of Rio, Chile, Buenos Aires and Cape Horn. Ocean Cruise Line's video, "Scandinavia Holidays," contains beautiful footage narrated by a couple reminiscing about their cruise. Its Mediterranean video includes footage of ports of call in the Mediterranean. These 12 to 20-minute tapes are approximately $7 each and will give you valuable information on cruise lines, their itineraries and the ports of call.

CLIA's tour and land library consists of videotapes with destinations such as Hawaii, Brazil and Alaska. These tapes are actual tour operator itineraries. For example, Abercrombie and Kent's "Into Africa" covers safaris in the style and luxury associated with Abercrombie and Kent. Maupintour highlights its "New England Fall Foliage Tour" by capturing the beauty of autumn colors in New England. The Hawaiian Island "overview" covers all five islands, highlights the islands' beautiful scenery and provides information on tourist attractions and places to stay. Averaging $5 – $9 each, these land and tour videos will give you a visual feel for an area.

For more information on obtaining these videos contact Vacations on Video, 7642 E. Gray Road, Suite 103, Scottsdale, AZ 85260, Telephone (602) 483-1551, Fax (602) 483-0785.

For information about a CLIA membership or to order a cruise manual, contact CLIA at 500 Fifth Avenue, Suite 1407, New York, NY 10110, Telephone (212) 921-0066, Fax (212) 921-0549.

People

Your Tour Operator's Operations Agent

Operations agents, who are employed by tour operators to handle details of the cruise, are usually familiar with the ship and its itinerary as well as any problems that may have arisen with passengers during the booking of the cruise. They have much of the information you need about your particular cruise and are excellent resources for you to use. They also should be able to provide you with the ship's diagrams and shore excursion books.

Cruise Hosts Who Have Previously Sailed on Your Ship or Cruise

Cruise hosts who have worked on your cruise before are often your best sources of information. They often have established a good rapport with the officers and other on-board staff members. This can smooth the way for your first cruise. However, take what other cruise hosts say with a grain of salt — they may have encountered problems you won't, and personalities sometimes clash. They will be familiar with which public rooms are best for cocktail parties, office hours and other special functions, the ports, shore excursions, what facilities are available at the dock, and where to find shopping areas, restaurants and special attractions.

Do your homework first, however. It is not fair to expect a cruise host to brief you on things you can research yourself. Call them only after you have done your homework. Most cruise hosts will be happy to provide a cruise briefing as a professional courtesy. A small gift or other compensation is appropriate for this service.

Books and Publications

Travel Books Purchased in Foreign Countries

In addition to whatever travel books you buy at home, you can usually purchase better books written in the country you are visiting — books that are not available in the United States. They often have more detailed photos and maps. (These purchases may qualify as a tax-deductible business expense.)

Culturgrams

"Culturgrams," four-page reports on various countries, are produced by Brigham Young University. They are referred to as "people maps" because they present a country's people — including their values, customs, and cultural assumptions, traditions and lifestyles. Topics included in these four-page profiles are:

- Customary methods of expressing greetings
- General attitudes of the people
- The population and its characteristics
- Language
- Religion
- Diet and traditional foods
- Land and climate
- Dating and marriage
- History and government
- Education and literacy
- Useful words and phrases
- Transportation and communication
- Map of the country

You can purchase the culturgram series of 102 countries for approximately $40, which includes shipping and handling. If you want to order culturgrams of individual countries, they are available for about $1 each, including shipping. You can also write for a free brochure listing countries and prices (discounts for multiple copies). The culturgrams are updated yearly and the new additions are available in March. New countries are added with each yearly update. For more information contact Publications Services, David M. Kennedy Center for International Studies, Brigham Young University, 280 HRCB, Provo, UT 84602, Telephone (801) 378-6528.

Culturgrams are also available in two bound books. Volume One is *The Americas and Europe*. Volume Two is *Africa, Asia and Oceania*. These books are available only from Garrett Park Press, P.O. Box 190, Garrett Park, MD 20896, Telephone (301) 946-2553. Each volume is approximately $19, payable by check or money order. These volumes are also updated annually.

The Weissmann Travel Report

This compact travel resource and destination information book is filled with wonderful information on hundreds of domestic and international areas. Each area covered starts out with a map of the country or city, followed by:

- Introduction to the area
- Main attractions
- What to do (in each major city of a country)
- Geostats (geographic statistics)
- Sample tour itineraries
- Where to go
- Transportation
- Accommodations
- Health advisories
- What to buy
- What to eat
- Do's and don'ts
- Potpourri
- Review questions about the country

The books come in three-ring binders, which allow for adding updates. The information is candid, complete and to the point. It tells the inside story of what is going on in travel destinations and the pros and cons about each destination. Miscellaneous information (airport/city codes, time changes, glossary, etc.) is also included. With a slogan of "we tell all," it is known as *the* destination reference in the travel industry.

The Weissmann Travel Report is available only through subscription. The International Profile (1200 destinations) is approximately $299 for the first year with yearly renewal fees of $135. The U.S. and Canada book (900 destinations) is $269 for the initial subscription with a yearly renewal fee of $135. Updates are done three times a year at which time approximately 25 international countries and 19 domestic areas are replaced. For more information, or to order the Weissmann Travel Report, contact them at Travel Report Associates, P.O. Box 49279, Austin, TX 78765, Telephone (512) 320-8700.

Selling Destinations by Marc Mancini
(Department of Travel, West Los Angeles College)

This is a new publication that approaches geography from a travel industry perspective. It is targeted to those who, as Mancini says, *sell* destinations. Chapters cover North America, Latin America, Europe, Africa, the Middle East, Asia, Australia and the South Pacific. Each chapter contains:

- Maps
- Climate charts (temperature, rainfall)
- Summary of geographic facts (history, language, currency)
- Cultural notes
- Reference books, videotapes and useful contact organizations
- Recommended places to visit within given regions
- Sample itineraries and local transportation
- Lodging options
- Tips to give clients
- Sales strategies
- Travel trivia
- Highlights of the most popular sights in each area

This 485-page book is comprehensive, readable, well-designed and well-indexed. Although directed to the travel professional who sells travel, this book contains a lot of valuable information for a professional cruise host.

Selling Destinations is not available in book stores. For information or to place an order, contact Van Nostrand Reinhold/Wadsworth, 7625 Empire Drive, Florence, KY 41042, Telephone (800) 354-9706.

Miscellaneous Resource Material
"Freebies"

While browsing in the ports (or while on pre- and post-cruise tours), pick up free newspapers, travel books, magazines and maps. If time permits, visit the tourist information bureaus in each area and collect the brochures they offer. Many have a location on or near the cruise ship dock. Look for local maps. They often have more detailed maps than are available through their government tourist offices in the United States.

Shore Excursion Brochure

If your tour operator has not provided you with a shore excursion brochure, call the cruise line's sales department directly. Advise the sales staff that you are a cruise host. Give your tour operator's name and the ship and cruise on which you will be bringing a group. Then say, "Since I have not been on this itinerary (or ship) before, it would be helpful if I could get a copy of the shore excursions so I can brief my clients." Cruise lines are very good about sending this information. Call the cruise line directly *only as a last resort.*

Ship's Diagrams (deck chart)

Your tour operator should have a diagram of the ship for you but, if not, you can find one in the brochures advertising the ship's itineraries. The CLIA manual also has updated cruise line ship's diagrams for member ships.

Ship's Newspaper

The ship's newspaper *(Example 1.1)* is a valuable resource. Keep back copies in your files. From the newspaper you can gather such information as:

- Ship's daily activities
- Dress for the day (formal, informal, casual)
- Disembarkation information
- Approximate time of arrival in ports
- Approximate times tours usually depart
- Whether meals have open or assigned seating
- Which ports use tenders and what decks they will depart from
- Briefings on the ports
- Maps
- Currency exchange rates
- Time zone changes

Reviewing the ship's paper will be helpful when you prepare your own handouts (see chapter 4). Remember, you don't want to duplicate the ship's

Monday at Sea   (Dress: Formal)

6:30 a.m.	Early Bird Coffee	Pastorale Cafe
8:00 a.m.	Pool & Whirlpools Open	Boheme/Daphne Deck
8:00 a.m.	Sports Deck Opens - Ping Pong, Basketball	Electra Deck Aft
8:00 a.m.	Shuffleboard	Aida Deck
8:00 a.m.	Walk a Mile with a Smile (6 laps = 1 mile)	Daphne Deck
9:00 a.m.	Cruisercise Program	Royal Fireworks Lounge
9:00 a.m.	Skeet Shooting	Electra Deck Aft
9:30 a.m.	Complimentary Snorkel Lessons	Daphne Deck Aft-Pool
10:00 a.m.	Slot Machines Open	Carmen Deck
10:00 a.m.-12:00 noon	Cards & Games Available	Harmony Room
10:00 a.m.	Morning Movie	Intermezzo Theater
10:30 a.m.	Port Review on Grand Cayman & Montego Bay with your Cruise Director	Carmen Lounge
11:30 a.m.	Horse Racing - The Sport of Kings (Win a Fortune with the Horses)	Carmen Lounge
12:00 noon-2:30 p.m.	Calypso Music on Deck	Carmen Deck Aft
1:00 p.m.	Underwater Video Presentation "Our Underwater World"	Intermezzo Theater
1:30 p.m.	Complimentary Snorkel Lessons	Daphne Deck Aft-Pool
2:00 p.m.-3:00 p.m.	Cruise Staff Hospitality Desk Cards, Games and Books Available	Harmony Room
2:00 p.m.	Casino Opens	Carmen Deck
2:00 p.m.	Black Jack and Roulette Lessons	Surprise Casino
2:00 p.m.	Afternoon Movie	Intermezzo Theater
2:00 p.m.	Fashion Show	Pastorale Cafe
2:15 p.m.	Card Players Meet	Harmony Room
2:30 p.m.	Scuba Lessons "Dry"	Prelude Bar
2:30 p.m.	Pool Games with Cruise Staff	LaMer Pool
2:30 p.m.	Dance Class	Carmen Lounge
3:00 p.m.	Wine Tasting (nominal charge)	Royal Fireworks Lounge
3:00 p.m.	Scavenger Quest	Carmen Lounge
3:30 p.m.	Scuba Demonstration	Daphne Deck Aft-Pool
4:00 p.m.	Snowball Bingo	Carmen Lounge
5:15 p.m.-6:00 p.m. 1st Sitting 7:15 p.m.-8:00 p.m. 2nd Sitting	**CAPTAIN'S WELCOME ABOARD RECEPTION** *The Captain Cordially Invites all Passengers* *to this Special Cocktail Party held in their Honor*	Carmen Lounge
7:30 p.m.-8:15 p.m.	Music for your Enjoyment	Royal Fireworks Lounge
8:30 p.m. 1st Sitting 10:30 p.m. 2nd Sitting	**LET THE STARS COME OUT** • • • SHOWTIME • • •	Carmen Lounge
9:30 p.m.-1:30 a.m.	Music for your Listening & Dancing Pleasure	Royal Fireworks Lounge
9:30 p.m.-12:00 a.m.	Piano Bar Opens	Serenade Bar
10:00 p.m.	Evening Movie	Intermezzo Theater
10:00 p.m.-3:00 a.m.	The Agitato Disco is Open	Fidelio Deck Aft
12:00 a.m.-1:00 a.m.	Crepes Flambes Buffet	Bacchanalia Restaurant

Example 1.1 Ship's Newspaper

information. You will use the ship's paper to be aware of what is going on in a general way, to get ideas for elaborating on your port letters and to assure that your scheduled activities do not conflict with those of the ship.

If the ship or cruise is new to you, ask a cruise host who has worked on the ship before, or your tour operator, for past copies of the paper. If your tour operator doesn't have any, suggest that a file be started.

World Atlas by The Software Toolworks

Although the World Atlas is a computer program that requires you to run your own printouts, I feel it should be included here. In addition to the wonderful maps you can access, it also provides eleven major informational categories with over 300 subtopics of interest for each country including:

- Travel (14 topics)
- Geography (15 topics)
- People (35 topics)
- Education (15 topics)
- Health (25 topics)
- Government (23 topics)
- Crime (14 topics)
- Economy (51 topics)
- Agriculture (79 topics)
- Communications (18 topics)
- International Organizations (125 topics)

This software is available for IBM and Macintosh. Annual updates will be available. For more information, contact The Software Toolworks, 60 Leveroni Court, Novato, CA 94949, Telephone (415) 883-3000.

MapArt

MapArt is another computer program. It was used to create the outline map of South America *(Example 4.5)*. This program, available for Mac and IBM, provides presentation quality clip art maps and can be obtained for International and United States destinations. For more information contact MicroMaps Software, 9 Church Street, P.O. Box 757, Lambertville, NJ 08530.

These are just some of the many research resources available to you. Don't be overwhelmed. You won't use them all. You will quickly discover your personal favorites. Just remember, proper research is the key to a successful tour. And, it is also a lot of fun.

Chapter 2

Assembling Documents

As the tour operator's business agent, you need to assemble various documents, which the tour operator should provide. Ideally, they should be in your hands at least a week before embarkation day but be prepared to get them as late as a day or two prior to the cruise. In any case, you need these documents so you can prepare all the paperwork that assures a successful experience for all concerned.

These documents fall into two categories:

- Booking documents the cruise line supplies to the tour operator
- Documents the tour operator independently supplies to the cruise host

---

From the Cruise Line
Passenger Invoices

Obviously each cruise line's invoice varies. It may be one invoice for each cabin (*Example 2.1*) or one long computer printout for the entire group (*Example 2.2*).

Example 1.1 is a passenger invoice by cabin, showing two people in one cabin. It contains the following information:

- Name of the cruise
- Booking number
- Passengers' names
- Cruise fare category
- Cabin numbers assigned
- Group fare
- Taxes paid
- Cancellation fee (trip cancellation insurance)
- Total amount paid for the cruise.

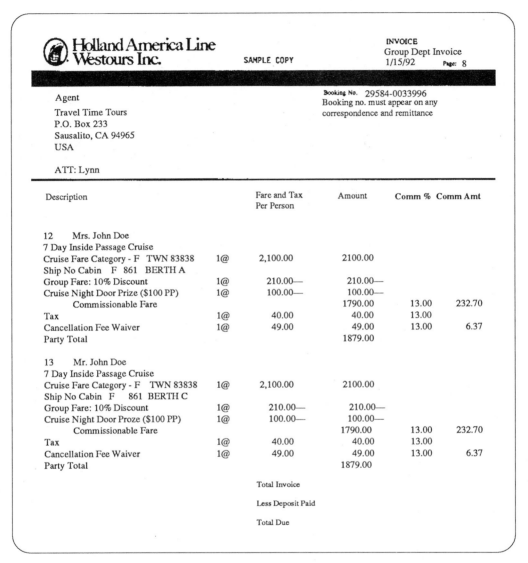

Holland America Line Westours Inc.

SAMPLE COPY

INVOICE
Group Dept Invoice
1/15/92   Page: 8

Agent

Travel Time Tours
P.O. Box 233
Sausalito, CA 94965
USA

ATT: Lynn

Booking No.   29584-0033996
Booking no. must appear on any
correspondence and remittance

Description		Fare and Tax Per Person	Amount	Comm %	Comm Amt
12 Mrs. John Doe					
7 Day Inside Passage Cruise					
Cruise Fare Category - F TWN 83838	1@	2,100.00	2100.00		
Ship No Cabin F 861 BERTH A					
Group Fare: 10% Discount	1@	210.00—	210.00—		
Cruise Night Door Prize ($100 PP)	1@	100.00—	100.00—		
Commissionable Fare			1790.00	13.00	232.70
Tax	1@	40.00	40.00	13.00	
Cancellation Fee Waiver	1@	49.00	49.00	13.00	6.37
Party Total			1879.00		
13 Mr. John Doe					
7 Day Inside Passage Cruise					
Cruise Fare Category - F TWN 83838	1@	2,100.00	2100.00		
Ship No Cabin F 861 BERTH C					
Group Fare: 10% Discount	1@	210.00—	210.00—		
Cruise Night Door Proze ($100 PP)	1@	100.00—	100.00—		
Commissionable Fare			1790.00	13.00	232.70
Tax	1@	40.00	40.00	13.00	
Cancellation Fee Waiver	1@	49.00	49.00	13.00	6.37
Party Total			1879.00		
		Total Invoice			
		Less Deposit Paid			
		Total Due			

Example 2.1 Passenger Invoice by Cabin

Example 2.2 shows a computer printout for the entire group. Notice that on the same line as the passenger's name is the booking number (the cruise line's locating number), cabin number and cabin category for that reservation (e.g., John & Mary Doe, 345610-M-457). In addition to the names of each passenger in the group, this form shows the following individual breakdown:

- Names of passengers in each cabin booked for the group
- Product fare
- Group discount
- Net cruise fare (group fare less the discount)
- Airfare city, client's departure city (for air/sea packages). "Cruise Only" means the tour operator purchased the cruise package, without airfare from the cruise line.
- Total Options
- Taxes
- Booked amount — gross price of cruise
- Agency commission, amount paid and balance due

GROUP INVOICE   Page 1

Travel Time Tours   SS Blue Seas   6 APR FROM: HONOLULU   TO: Honolulu
P.O. Box 233   PRODUCT: 7 Day Cruise
Sausalito, CA 94965   GROUP #:   787966

ATT: John   AGENT #:   SF 4153311808

PASSENGER NAME

PRODUCT FARE	GROUP DISC	NET CRUISE FARE	AIR FARE/ CITY	TOTAL OPTIONS	TAXES	BOOKED AMOUNT	AGENCY COMM	AMT PAID	BALANCE DUE
Doe, Mr John/Mary			345610	BK M -457					
4000.00	700.00-	3300.00	Cruise Only	50.00	96.00	3446.00	325.00	3121.00	.00
Smith, Mr Sue/Bill			345611	BK M -579					
3900.00	650.00-	3250.00	Cruise Only	50.00	96.00	3396.00	325.00	3071.00	.00
Wall, Ms Barbara/Bell, Ms. Marsha			345612	BK A -295					
3900.00	650.00-	3250.00	Cruise Only	50.00	96.00	3396.00	325.00	3071.00	.00
Scott, Mr Bob/Homes, Ms Helen			345613	BK D -368					
4000.00	700.00-	3300.00	Cruise Only	50.00	96.00	3446.00	325.00	3121.00	.00

Example 2.2 Passenger Invoice by Group

The cruise line also forwards to the tour operator all cruise and airline tickets the passenger needs to board the ship (including yours). Along with the tickets is information on shore excursions, on-board activities and medical insurance coverage. The tour operator forwards these documents directly to each client. You will receive only your individual packet.

From the Tour Operator
Passenger Information

Some tour operators prefer not to send a cruise host actual copies of the cruise line invoices. In this case, the company should still provide you with the following information for each passenger in your group:

- Passenger's name and address
- Cruise line
- Cruise dates
- Ship's name
- Total cost of the cruise per passenger
- Category of cabin paid for, Berth (A or B) and cabin number
- Booking number
- Name(s) of other person(s) in cabin
- Extra amenities the tour operator contracted for
- Flight departure city and airfare paid
- Pre-or post-cruise tours (extended tour packages the client has booked)
- Trip cancellation waiver paid for or declined (important to know in case your client must leave the cruise early because of illness, injury or death in the family)
- Port taxes (added to stateroom bills if they are not paid in advance; if they appear on a client's bill, you will need to know whether the tour operator has prepaid them)
- Prepaid shore excursions (which excursions scheduled and amounts paid)
- Total amount due
- Meal requests: Late seating/smoking/table for eight/diabetic/special low-salt meals required/wheelchair for shore excursions/birthday or anniversary
- T/W (traveling with)

Cocktail Party Arrangements

During negotiations with the cruise line, the tour operator usually asks whether the ship can provide a complimentary cocktail party for the clients. Some ships automatically provide a party when there are 30 or more paying passengers in the group. Some will do it with fewer passengers if the request is made by the tour operator or if booked well in advance. Details of such a prearranged function should be forwarded to you. These should include any food service to be provided and a tipping schedule for the waiters and bartender.

Problem-Passenger Reports

It would be very useful if tour operators would provide their cruise hosts with reports on problem passengers *(Example 2.3)*; however, most don't. Problem passengers may be those who were difficult during the booking process or who had legitimate problems with ticketing for flights, and so on. Knowing about these problems before you meet your clients makes you better able to deal with their dissatisfactions and allows you to prepare yourself with ways to turn an angry client around. (Depending on how you handle the situation, your most difficult client could turn out to be your nicest passenger.)

Problem Passenger

NAME: Bill Jones

PROBLEM: Bill was upset because he was not allowed to deviate from the scheduled cruise line itinerary flight. He chose to make his own travel arrangements. In doing so he found that the price of the airfare was double and he was not able to get the flights he wanted. He felt that our agency should have been able to get him the flight changes and rate he requested. We were not able to do this since the cruise line does not allow any deviations. He is very angry.

TOUR OPERATOR SOLUTION: We offered to re-book his flight through the cruise line, accepting the original schedule. He declined and is still making the arrangements on his own. We expect he will be very un-happy when he boards.

CRUISE HOST REPORT (Fill in how you handled this problem)

_____

_____

_____

_____

Date: _____ Cruise Host: _____

Example 2.3 Problem-Passenger Report

Not only do such reports assist you to establish good relationships with your clients but they also protect you from complaints that may appear on the client end-of-cruise evaluations.

Confidential Client Information Sheets

In addition to providing you with general passenger booking information, the tour operator should have requested confidential client information from all passengers and provided it to you. *Example 2.4* shows what points are generally included. This information will be invaluable throughout the cruise.

- Photograph — a photograph of each client will help you learn names and faces before meeting your clients on the ship. When you greet them by name, they feel very special. This type of personal recognition and service makes a lasting impression on your clients.

- Name and address

- Telephone number

- Marital status

- Birth date

- Occupation — useful as a topic for discussion and for introductions.

- Hobbies or interests — useful for general conversation, for introducing people with similar interests and for informing people of activities that may be of interest to them either on ship or in port.

- Celebrating a birthday or anniversary

- Confidential information box — which includes health and medical conditions that you as cruise host may need to know in case of emergencies.

- Smoker/nonsmoker

- In case of emergency — very important that you know whom to contact in case of illness or death.

Tipping Policy

The tour operator usually establishes a tipping (or non-tipping) policy for their clients to follow and outlines their policy in their brochure or in the final cruise documents. The clients will have received this information before they arrive on board. Typically, such notification looks like this:

Travel Time Tours

Please attach a recent photograph to help the cruise host identify you.
Photos will be returned upon your request.

Travel Time Tours thanks you for participating in your upcoming tour. You can help us make your trip a pleasant and safe one by providing the information below. Your cruise host will keep this information confidential and will use it only as circumstances require. Please complete and return the form at your earliest convenience. Thank you.

Please complete (print) one form per person

Name: _____

Street Address: _____

City: _____ State: _____ Zip: _____

Telephone Number (   ) _____

Marital Status _____ Date of Birth _____

Occupation: _____   _____ Smoker   _____ Nonsmoker

Hobbies or interests _____

While traveling will you be celebrating a birthday ?_____ anniversary ?_____ Date: _____

IN CASE OF EMERGENCY:

Please provide medical information:

Check all that apply and explain, if necessary:

Special dietary requirements	
Diabetes	
Heart problems	
Respiratory problems	
Allergies	
Difficulty walking	
Difficulty hearing	
Difficulty seeing	
Do you require a wheelchair?	
List medications you are presently taking:	

Please notify:

Name: _____

Relationship: _____

Address: _____

City: _____

State: _____ Zip: _____

Telephone: Home (   ) _____

Business   (   ) _____

Example 2.4 Confidential Client Information Form

An end-of-cruise gratuity to your cruise host is appropriate as an expression of your appreciation for services rendered. A gratuity to the cruise host has not been included in the price of your cruise. As a guideline, we suggest a minimum of $10-$15 per person for a cruise of 7 days, $15-$20 per person up to 15 days, and $20-$30 per person for cruises longer than 15 days.

It is appropriate to ask your company whether your clients have received tipping information.

Client End-of-Cruise Evaluation Forms

End-of-cruise evaluation forms may be provided for you to hand out to passengers before their final disembarkation. These evaluations allow the tour operator to verify the effectiveness of the planning, operational and customer-relations aspects of the cruise. They also let the company know how well clients were treated and what areas need improvement. The tour operator uses this information in planning future tours. Important to you, of course, is that the tour operator will also use this information to assess your performance as cruise host. A typical evaluation form is shown in *Example 2.5*.

Miscellaneous Documents

There are several other documents the tour operator should forward to you as a cruise host. They are:

- Enough copies of the group passenger list (names and addresses) to provide one for each client
- Various other report forms you are required to complete and return to the tour operator's office — for example, a general summary of the cruise, expense reports, accident and death reports, problem-passenger reports
- Tour operator 24-hour contact numbers in case of emergency
- Information on any trip cancellation insurance the tour operator or cruise line provides, including the details of what is covered (damaged or lost luggage, medical problems, trip cancellation, etc.).
- List of pre- and post-tour clients
- Names and telephone numbers of other cruise hosts who have worked on the ship or have taken the same cruise
- Copies of the ship's daily newspaper, if available
- Extra confidential client information sheets (in case clients have not returned theirs to the tour operator).

Travel Time Tours
CLIENT END-OF-CRUISE EVALUATION

Passenger name _____

Address _____

City/State/Zip _____ Phone _____

Tour code # _____ Destination _____ Date _____

Is this your first cruise?   Y ☐   N ☐

If not, how many times (including this cruise) have you sailed?_____

Have you sailed on this ship before?   Y ☐   N ☐

Have you sailed with this cruise line before?   Y ☐   N ☐

Why did you choose this ship? _____

_____

This itinerary? _____

_____

_____

PLEASE RATE THE FOLLOWING

	Excellent	Very Good	Good	Fair	Poor
Overall cleanliness of ship	☐	☐	☐	☐	☐
Cabin cleanliness	☐	☐	☐	☐	☐
Cabin steward service	☐	☐	☐	☐	☐
Service in dining room	☐	☐	☐	☐	☐
Quality of food	☐	☐	☐	☐	☐
Service in cocktail lounges	☐	☐	☐	☐	☐
Quality of drinks	☐	☐	☐	☐	☐
Service on deck	☐	☐	☐	☐	☐
Ship's amenities	☐	☐	☐	☐	☐
Ship's entertainment	☐	☐	☐	☐	☐
Ship's social staff	☐	☐	☐	☐	☐
Ship's cruise director	☐	☐	☐	☐	☐
Boutiques	☐	☐	☐	☐	☐
Cruise host	☐	☐	☐	☐	☐
Overall cruise experience	☐	☐	☐	☐	☐

Page 1

Example 2.5 Client End-of-Cruise Evaluation Form

REGARDING SHORE EXCURSIONS

Did you like the selections?   Y☐   N☐

Did you get value for your money?   Y☐   N☐

If not, which shore excursion did you not like and why? _____

_____

REGARDING THE CRUISE

What did you like best about the cruise? _____

_____

_____

What did you like least about the cruise? _____

_____

_____

Did you take a pre- or post-tour option?   Pre ☐   Post ☐

REGARDING YOUR CRUISE HOST

Was your cruise host friendly?   Y☐   N☐

Was your cruise host knowledgeable?   Y☐   N☐

Did you enjoy the functions provided by your cruise host?   Y☐   N☐

What function did you like best? _____

_____

Do you feel the handouts provided by your cruise host were valuable?   Y☐   N☐

Which handouts did you like best and why? _____

_____

Was there anything else the cruise host could have done to help make your trip more
pleasurable? _____

_____

_____

How many vacations do you take each year?_____

Will your next vacation be a   Cruise☐   Land tour ☐   Both ☐

What destination(s) do you plan to visit? _____

Is there any service you feel Travel Time Tours should have provided to you and did
not? _____

_____

Page 2

Example 2.5 Client End-of-Cruise Evaluation Form

Chapter 3

Developing Your Paperwork

The better you prepare for your cruise before you board the ship, the easier your job will be. It will allow you more time with your clients and for your personal enjoyment.

Your success as a cruise host will depend on: the quality of information you receive from the tour operator, the amount of time you devote to using the information, the amount of preparation you do and the working relationship you develop with the on-board staff. The last point is critical and will be discussed at length in chapter 10.

As soon as you receive the cruise documents from the tour operator, use the information to prepare the various lists, charts, forms and notices you will need at different points during the cruise. You can prepare them by hand, but the fastest and easiest way is with a computer. I used the *Cruise Hosting Computer Program* for the Macintosh (see appendix). Make enough copies of these documents for all of your clients and your personal needs for the entire cruise. (The ship's copying facilities are limited.) If possible, print notices on company stationery. If this is not possible, all notices should include some form of company identification as well as your own name and cabin number. The following are some suggestions on documents that would be helpful to have.

Lists, Charts, Forms, Notices
Rooming List by Cabin Number

A rooming list by cabin number (*Example 3.1*) provides you with a check-off sheet for delivering information and invitations to your clients as well as a "to-do" list you can fill out as you talk with them. If you have a small group you can usually get to know each person by name. However, if you have a larger group you can ask clients for their cabin numbers and quickly run down the numerically arranged list to find their names. Remember that, at best, it usually takes a few days to learn all your clients' names. Asking for a cabin number is often less offensive.

Cabin #	Name	Comments
A111	Smith, Jim Smith, Barbara	
D345	Evans, Bob Evans, Evelyn	
M555	Flower, Mary Katz, Betty	

Example 3.1 Rooming List by Cabin Number

Dining Room Seating Request Chart

Clients often request first (also called main) or second (also called late) seating. Sometimes the tour operator will request one seating for the entire group. Either way, your tour operator should provide you with seating request information.

If a dining room seating request chart *(Example 3.2)* has not been provided by the tour operator, create one yourself using the following criteria. Take the information you have for each client and group them by:

- Cabin Number
- Name
- First or second seating
- Table size
- Smoking or non-smoking
- Traveling with
- Table number assigned

Having your dining room seating requests completed prior to meeting the maitre d' makes it easier to confirm final arrangements when you meet with him on board the first day. At that time, you can easily enter the table numbers the maitre d' assigns to your clients.

Cabin #	Name	Seating	Table Size	Smoking	Traveling with	Table #
A111	Smith	First	8	No	Jones	
A111	Smith	First	8	No	Jones	
I345	Evans	Second	4	No	Davis	
I345	Evans	Second	4	No	Davis	
I347	Davis	Second	4	No	Evans	
I347	Davis	Second	4	No	Evans	
M555	Dane	Second	6	Yes		
M555	Dane	Second	6	Yes		

Example 3.2 Dining Room Seating Request Chart

Group Dining Request Form

After you have talked with the maitre d' you will have all the information necessary to complete a formal Group Dining Request Form (*Example 3.3*). Insert the table numbers the maitre d' has assigned to your passengers. This form will be invaluable when you do your table rounds during dinner and will provide a helpful aid in learning your client's names.

Birthday and Anniversary List

At your first meeting with the maitre d' you will also want to provide him with a separate list of birthdays and anniversaries (*Example 3.4*), especially noting those clients celebrating a birthday or anniversary on the day of embarkation. (These events are usually celebrated on the following day.) Your list should provide date, event, cabin number, dinner seating, name of person(s) celebrating as well as a place to write in the client's table number. It's best to prepare the event list by date rather than by cabin number in case the cruise line has changed a cabin without your knowledge. (The maitre d' should, however, inform you of any cabin changes.)

Event Date	Event	Cabin #	Seating	Table #	Name
Wed, July 10	Birthday	A111	First		Jim Smith
Fri, July 12	Anniversary	D347	Second		David & Doris Davis

Example 3.4 Birthday and Anniversary List

GROUP DINING REQUEST

GROUP # _____ AGENCY _____

SAILING DATE _____ SHIP _____

NO. PASSENGERS _____

SEATING	CABIN #	PASSENGER NAME	REQUEST	REMARKS B-DAY /ANNIV /DIET
	A444	1. Harry Smith		12/1- Anniversary
FIRST	A444	2. Betty Smith	TABLE OF	
X	M356	3. John Arnold	# __8__	Low- salt Diet
	M356	4. Mary Arnold		
SECOND	O123	5. Angie White	SMOKING	
____	O123	6. Jill Simpson	____	12/5 - Birthday
		7.	NON SMOKING	
		8.	X	
	TABLE # 27			

SEATING	CABIN #	PASSENGER NAME	REQUEST	REMARKS B-DAY / ANNIV / DIET
		1.		
FIRST		2.	TABLE OF	
____		3.	# _____	
		4.		
SECOND		5.	SMOKING	
____		6.	____	
		7.	NON SMOKING	
		8.		
	TABLE #			

Example 3.3 Group Dining Request Form

The maitre d' may already have received this birthday and anniversary information from the cruise line office, but often it is incomplete. Preparing this form will show him that you are a professional. He will greatly appreciate your organization and the special attention you are showing your group.

Client List for Pre- and Post-Cruise Tours

Along with your cruise documents, your tour operator should have included a passenger list and itinerary of the pre- and post-cruise tours *(Example 3.5)*. The itinerary gives you information about the sights that will be seen in the areas visited. You may want to prepare written information and maps for those clients participating in post-tour travel.

Not all clients take these optional pre- or post-cruise tours. But for those who do, this information is very important for you to have. Cruise clients expect you to know their complete travel plans; when you don't, they lack confidence in you and your company.

Pre Destination Singapore	Post Destination Hong Kong	Cabin #	Name
	Y	D345	Bob Evans
	Y	D 345	Evelyn Evans
	Y	D347	David Davis
	Y	D347	Dora Davis
Y		A111	Jim Smith
Y		A111	Barbara Smith
Y		M555	Mary Flower

Example 3.5 Pre- and Post-Cruise Tour List

It is strongly suggested that you research pre- and post-cruise tour itineraries in preparation for questions your clients may have. It will also give you topics for discussion during the cruise. It is also important to be aware, for example, of whether your clients are coming from a pre-cruise tour where problems with sanitation, water or food may have been encountered. In addition, flights can be delayed in some locales because of airline problems or political unrest. The same is true for post-cruise tours.

The tour operator is not always financially able to include a cruise host on pre- or post-cruise tours. When the tour is to a difficult travel area, however, tour operators do a disservice to their companies, their cruise hosts and especially their clients by not including the cruise host on these tours.

I was once assigned a cruise to South America for which the cruise line provided a pre-cruise package to Peru. Five of my 120 passengers took this pre-cruise package. Many problems arose on the tour concerning flights, hotels, food and sickness, but no representative from my company was available to assist my clients. Luckily for the passengers, a cruise host from another company was on the tour, and he chose to help my passengers, getting them back to Argentina in time to board the ship. Although I commended him for assisting my clients, problems were created for me as a result. For the duration of the cruise my passengers went to the other cruise host with their questions and concerns; they were simply continuing the bond with him because he was there when they needed help. They were merely polite to me. And, although I provided the same services to these clients as to the rest of my passengers, at the end of the cruise the other cruise host received a big gratuity and I received a thank you!

Party Invitations

Some tour operators provide cocktail parties (bon voyage, welcome and/or farewell) for their clients. Sometimes the cruise line will provide a complimentary cocktail party for your group. It depends on the tour operator you work for and what pre-arrangements have been made with the cruise line.

If your tour operator is providing a cocktail party they may also provide preprinted invitations (*Example 3.6*). Sometimes complete cocktail party details have already been arranged by your tour operator before the departure date. In that case, you will have all the information needed to write the entire invitation. If the tour operator is unable to set the time and place before departure, however, you can still partially prepare invitations before you leave home, filling in the type of party (e.g., welcome or farewell), suggested dress (casual or formal) and your name as party host. (Be sure to use the same pen when you finish the invitations on board ship. It looks more professional).

You can also address the envelopes with your clients' names. For easy delivery, you can write the cabin number in the upper right-hand corner of the envelopes. Because the cruise line sometimes upgrades passengers at the last minute, it is best not to fill in cabin numbers until you can confirm them on board ship.

Travel Time Tours
Invites You to a

Welcome Party

Hosted by _____ *Cruise Host Name* _____

Date _____

Time _____

Place _____

Dress _____ *Casual* _____

Example 3.6 Tour Operator Cocktail Party Invitation

The pleasure of your company is requested

on _____ *between* _____

for cocktails in _____

Best Regards,

Example 3.7 Ship's Invitation

If your company does not provide preprinted invitations, the cruise director, bar manager or social staff can provide you with generic invitations with the ship's logo (*Example 3.7*).

"Office Hours" Notice

Plan to hold office hours (usually two hours each day) during the days you are at sea. This is the time especially set aside for your clients to discuss their questions or concerns, get help with any problems they may have or discuss their likes and dislikes about the cruise.

Before you leave home, prepare office hours notices (*Example 3.8*) for each day you will be at sea. Print the dates directly on the notices; leave the time blank until you have confirmed it with the ship's staff. Leave the place blank unless you have been on that ship before and know exactly where you want to hold your office hours.

For more information on holding office hours, see chapter 7, Maintaining Contact with Your Group.

Travel Time Cruise Members
Office Hours

I will be holding **OFFICE HOURS** at the following time and place. Please feel free to stop by and talk to me about any questions or concerns you might have, shore excursions and ports of call, future Travel Time tours, or just stop by to say hello!

DATE: Wednesday, September 8
TIME:
PLACE: Calypso Lounge

I look forward to seeing you there.

Cruise Host Name
Travel Time Cruise Host
Cabin#

Example 3.8 Office Hours Notice

Shore Excursion Itinerary

Using the ship's shore excursion brochure, highlight all the attractions to see or visit on shore excursion tours (*Example 3.9*). This way you can research the highlighted material for your briefing. (See chapter 6 for more information on content and timing of shore excursion briefings).

MONTEVIDEO • City Tour • 4 hours • $12

Uruguay's attractive capital combines superb examples of Spanish-colonial architecture with a lively beach resort atmosphere. On this half-day sightseeing tour, you'll get a taste of both. Admire the elegant residential and diplomatic district of **El Prado** and visit the **Palace of Legislation**, the city's sumptuous congressional building. Photograph the famous **bronze statues of Jose Belloni**, which depict the earliest days of Uruguay's history when settlers came in on wagon trains. Enjoy the spectacular views of the city from **Montevideo Hill** where you will visit **General Artiga's Fort** and its **military museum**. Then ride along glorious **Pocitos Beach** to the fun-filled atmosphere of **Mercado del Puerto** with its many cafes, restaurants, shops and street musicians. Continue on to the **antique flea market of Zabala Square.**

Example 3.9 Shore Excursion Brochure: City Tour of Montevideo

Use the information you obtained from tourist bureaus, consulates and libraries (see chapter 1, Using Available Resources) for each attraction. Prepare a few descriptive paragraphs for every shore excursion so that during your briefing you will be able to paint a word picture of what clients can expect to see and experience. Include important briefing information you have received from other cruise hosts who have done the same itinerary before; for example (the first two are the two most commonly asked questions):

- Difficulty of the tour: Is the walking strenuous? Are there many stairs?
- How much time is allowed for shopping?
- Condition of coaches: Do they have air conditioning, a good sound system, restroom facilities? (Restroom facilities are important to be aware of, especially on longer shore excursion tours with older clients.)
- Are the guides easy to understand?
- Is the tour worth the price?
- Can clients see the area on their own?

Client End-of-Cruise Evaluation Forms

Sometimes the tour operator will require clients to mail end-of-cruise evaluation forms at the end of the cruise, but in many instances you will be collecting them. If you are collecting these evaluation forms (*Example 2.5*) put the form in an envelope with the client's name on the outside. After you are on board ship and you are sure of your clients' cabin numbers, put the number in the upper right-hand corner of each envelope. This procedure will speed delivery as well as allow you to check off which evaluations you've received and which you need to collect.

Cruise Data Sheet

A cruise data sheet (*Example 3.10*) lists important events occurring on the cruise, along with their dates, times and places. Some information — the time of the mandatory boat drill, cruise staff introductions and shore excursion talks — you can get from the ship's newspaper if the event occurs on the day of boarding. Get the rest of the information during your initial meeting with the cruise director, who will usually know all the times and dates for repeaters' parties; captain's parties; galley, bridge, and engine room tours; talent night; masquerade night; shore excursion talks; and snowball jackpot bingo. Most ships have the same or similar activities. You can add or delete information as you feel necessary.

Once you've confirmed all ship's activities, you can schedule your own at times that do not conflict with theirs. The cruise data sheet will be an important reference for you during the cruise.

CRUISE DATA SHEET

SHIP: SAILING DATE:
DESTINATION:
ARRIVAL: DEPARTURE:

	DATE	TIME	ROOM	DECK

Ship's Activities

Boat Drill
Shore Excursion Talk
Cruise Staff Introductions
Captain's Welcome Cocktail Party
Captain's Farewell Cocktail Party
Repeaters' Party
Talent Show
Masquerade
Ship's Bridge Tour
Ship's Galley Tour
Ship's Engine Room Tour
Tender Ports
Formal Nights
Disembarkation Briefing
Bingo

Cruise Host Scheduled Activities

First Briefing
Shore Excursion Briefing
Disembarkation Briefing
Special Briefing
Welcome Party
Farewell Party
Gathering Places
Private Bridge Tour
Private Galley Tour
Private Engine Room Tour
Office Hours
Special Activity
Special Activity

Example 3.10 Cruise Data Sheet

Ship's Diagram

Another useful document to have is a diagram of the ship (*Example 3.11*). Make a copy of the diagram and highlight (with a see-through marking pen) your clients' cabins. It will give you a better visual picture of cabin locations and be useful when you deliver information. It will also help you stay oriented. If you have not been on the ship before, it is easy to get turned around below deck. You will quickly learn tricks of the trade. For example, on some ships the even-numbered cabins are on the left as you face the bow (front) of the ship. "Left" has four letters and "even" has four letters. The left is also the port side — "port" also has four letters. You may also find that the port side of the ship has a different color carpet than the starboard side. Similarly, on some ships the elevator in the back may be gold-colored whereas the elevator toward the front of the ship may be silver. You can't depend on all of these applying to all ships, but take notice of these distinguishing marks, both for yourself and your clients.

Door Decorations

In a class by itself are door decorations. They are not only useful in identifying your clients' cabins and thus making delivery of handouts easier, they also serve as a good way to introduce yourself and your company.

Door decorations can be a picture that relates to the region you are cruising: for example, in Mexico, it could be a Mexican hat or a donkey; in Alaska, a whale or glacier; in China, an Asian face with a typical Chinese hat, or a pagoda. Cut these out of construction paper or simply make photocopies. Put these decorations on all your clients' cabin doors. These decorations can be small enough to leave up even if you later add a special holiday decoration. This is a simple and inexpensive way to advertise your company.

OCEAN PEARL

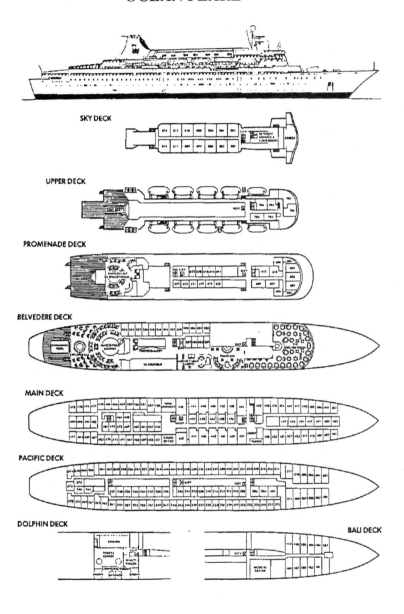

Example 3.11 Ship's Diagram

Chapter 4

Preparing Handouts

The handout is an important device for maintaining contact with your clients. They can be prepared before you leave home. Use your imagination and be as creative as you can in putting them together. Printing your handouts on distinctive, colored paper will help your clients easily distinguish them from the ship's information. Remember you do not have to produce all the documents suggested here. The following is a list of things you can do. Pick and choose the ones you feel will be useful to you.

Letters
Welcome Letter

A welcome letter does just that — it welcomes your clients to the cruise and introduces you to them. It discusses your first group meeting — called a briefing. (Refer to chapter 6 for more on briefings.) If the briefing has been prearranged by the tour operator, the time and place can be included.

Print your welcome letter on your tour operator's stationery or include some form of company identification. Your welcome letter should:

- Welcome your clients on board
- Introduce yourself as the cruise host
- Mention any other materials attached (passenger name list, for example)
- Advise the group of place, date and time of your initial briefing
- Note the importance of at least one member of the party attending the briefing
- Let them know you will be available the first day and where and how they can contact you
- Include your name and cabin number.

Have these letters ready to deliver on embarkation day. If you will be arranging your briefing time and place after you board the ship, hand-write the date, time and place on each copy before distributing.

September 6

DEAR TRAVEL TIME CRUISE MEMBER

Welcome aboard the beautiful S.S. *Dolphin*. My name is (cruise host name) and I will be your cruise host during this cruise to Nassau. I look forward to being with you. I know that sailing on the *Dolphin* will be an experience you will truly enjoy.

Our ports of call are **KEY WEST, FREEPORT, NASSAU,** and **BLUE LAGOON ISLAND**. You will find an abundance of sights to see and activities in which to participate. Or, just kick off your shoes, settle back, and bask in the warm ambiance of the Bahamas.

Enclosed is a list of your fellow passengers. You will have the opportunity to get acquainted with them at our briefing. (Time, date, and place is listed below.) It is important that at least one member of your family attend this briefing.
I look forward to meeting you and discussing the upcoming activities and shore excursions. I will also tell you about sea life on board the ship. Following the general briefing, I will be available for any questions you may have.

We will have our welcome party on Wednesday the 9th, and I will be sending you all an invitation. Enjoy your first day on the *Dolphin*. Get acquainted with the ship and get those sea legs working!

My cabin number is listed below. Please contact me if you need me.

Briefing Notice

Place: **Library**

Date: **Monday, Sept 7**

Time: **3:00 - 3:30 PM**

BON VOYAGE!

Cruise Host Name
Travel Time Cruise Host
Cabin #

Example 4.1 Welcome Letter for a Cruise in the Bahamas.
(The briefing time and place was prearranged.)

March 9

Dear Cruise Member:

Welcome aboard the beautiful *Royal Viking Sea*. My name is (cruise host name) and I will be your cruise host during this fabulous 15-day cruise. You have chosen a wonderful vacation. Australia and New Zealand are filled with friendly, easy-going people and some of the most beautiful scenery you will see anywhere in the world. You will be traveling in style aboard the *Royal Viking Sea*, and its crew is among the finest in the industry.

I will try to meet those of you whom I have not yet met and will be as visible as possible on the ship tonight to help you with questions or problems.

Your dining table request has been submitted to the cruise line. You will find a card in your cabin with your table number. On this ship there is only one seating, so everyone will eat at the same time. Please keep your assigned seating the first night.

If you have a problem with your table and would like to change, please let me know tonight after dinner, or tomorrow morning at our briefing. I will meet with the maitre d' and get it corrected for you. It is always easier to make changes the following day when the maitre d' has a little more time and knows what he has available.

Enclosed is a list of your fellow passengers. You will have the opportunity to get acquainted with them at our briefing. Time, date, and place will be listed on my Briefing Notice, which I will distribute later today. I look forward to seeing you there and discussing the upcoming activities and shore excursions. I will also tell you about sea life on board the ship. Following the general briefing, I will be available for any questions you may have. It is very important that *at least one member of your party* attend this briefing.

Thank you,

Cruise Host Name
Travel Time Cruise Host
Cabin #

Example 4.2 Welcome Letter without Briefing Information

If you cannot prearrange the briefing time, you must send a separate briefing notice after your welcome letter is delivered. (Your welcome letter should be delivered prior to your clients' arrival.) *Example 4.2* shows a welcome letter without briefing information. A separate briefing notice was distributed.

If you must send out a separate briefing notice (*Example 4.3*), include the following information:

- The purpose of the briefing
- Date, time, place
- Importance of at least one member of the party attending

Travel Time Cruise Members

Briefing Notice

We will be having a special Travel Time briefing at the time and place listed below. I have some important information to share with you about shipboard life, shore excursions, and special Travel Time activities. This briefing will also afford you an opportunity to meet your fellow Travel Time cruise members for the first time.

This meeting **SHOULD NOT BE MISSED.** It is important that at least one member of your party attend.

DATE:

TIME:

PLACE:

I look forward to seeing you there.

Cruise Host Name
Travel Time Cruise Host
Cabin #

Example 4.3 Separate Briefing Notice

Port Letters

Your own daily, personalized port letters, newsletters or cruise papers (whichever you prefer to call them) are good ways to keep in touch with your group. In general, port letters should cover the following information, as appropriate:

- History of the country or city

- Major sightseeing attractions, especially what should not be missed

- Survival information: Is the water safe to drink? Is the food safe to eat? Do drivers drive on the left or right? Is the crime rate high? What special precautions are advised?

- Money exchange: The name of the local currency and the current exchange rate (sometimes money can be exchanged on board ship.)

- Transportation: Information on taxis and public transportation

- Local public holidays: Holidays may mean that banks or shops will be closed or that a local holiday festival may be scheduled

- Shopping: Note anything that is a particularly good buy or that cannot be obtained elsewhere — specialty items such as coffee, perfume, hammocks and leather goods. Mention when the shops are open, especially if you are in a country that takes siestas. Mention items that can be obtained in the country but cannot be brought back into the United States (e.g., those made from alligator, snake, fur or endangered species, etc.)

- Time changes: If you will experience a time zone change, inform clients so they can reset their watches. You don't want anyone to miss the ship.

- Important foreign phrases: Include some useful phrases; for example, in addition to "please" and "thank you," "How much does this cost?" "How do I get back to the cruise ship dock?" "Where can I get a taxi?" If you will be calling at several ports in that country, create a separate handout (*Example 4.16*) listing these phrases so your clients can carry it with them while in each port. Spell the words phonetically for easier pronunciation. Not only will these phrases be helpful but enabling your passengers to communicate with the local people, even a little, is a wonderful experience for them.

Example 4.4 shows a port letter prepared before departure, using the resource material discussed in chapter 1.

Happy Birthday to Gail Smith!

April 4

CRUISE PAPER

SANTAREM (Sahn-tah-rain)

Santarem, a city of approximately 150,000, is the third largest town in the Amazon. In 1865 it was settled by white residents of South Carolina and Tennessee who had fled the Confederacy when slavery was abolished. After their arrival, Brazil permitted slavery for another 23 years. The Southerners still prospered and managed to build Santarem, which has become an important trading center for Brazil. It is where miners, gold prospectors, rubber tappers, and Brazil-nut gatherers pick up supplies. It is also an important supply center for the jute and lumber industries. Several bars display the Confederate flag. Many of the settlers' descendants still reside there. Many of them have since mixed with the Brazilians and have names like Jose Carlos Calhoun.

Santarem is not as sophisticated as Belem or Manaus but that is what gives it its charm. It is a typical small town with its winding, unpaved back streets, friendly slow-paced people and colonial architecture. The center of Santarem is its busy port, with lots of small fishing boats and dugout canoes.

Mercado Modelo is the open-air market in the center of town. This market is not as big as the market you will find in Belem, but it is well worth a visit. Here you will see local produce and people socializing. A good place to relax after shopping is along the eastern seawall, with its new walkway with benches and flowering shade trees to help keep you sheltered from the hot afternoon sun.

SANTAREM CITY TOUR
Natives don't speak English very well here. On the city tour there is no commentary or literature. The tour goes by the Tropical Hotel, then to the hammock factory (15-minute stop) where you will see how hammocks are made and will have an opportunity to shop. Hammocks cost from $5 to $21. Chair hammocks are $8. The tour then goes through town to the waterfront, with a stop in the center of town at the church (30 to 45 minutes will be given to walk around town). There are lots of shops: shoe stores, clothes, hammocks. You can see the ship from town. It is about a 45-minute walk back to the ship from town (maybe one hour). You can take a taxi back if you want more time to shop. **Coaches are not air conditioned.**

TROPICAL HOTEL: Has a pool and bar, three to five minutes from the ship.
TAXIS: Walk off the dock area and through the gate to get one.
SHOPPING: Hammocks downtown are half the price of those at the factory.

SEE YOU ON THE DOCK!

Cruise Host Name
TRAVEL TIME CRUISE HOST
Cabin #

DONT FORGET:
1. The sun will be very hot today. Use your sunscreen and take along a hat for protection.
2. I will look for you tonight at the "Buffet under the Stars". It starts at 11:00 pm by the pool on Ocean Deck.

Example 4.4 Port Letter

I have found it best to prepare the essentials of these letters at home, leaving space for special information to be added daily, once on board. The city map could be printed on the back. If you don't have time or prefer to create your port letters on board ship, I suggest taking along a portable typewriter or laptop computer and printer. Availability of typewriters and copiers is limited on most ships and nonexistent on others. If you have excellent penmanship, you can hand-write your port letters. If you choose this option, bring enough paper so you don't use the ship's supply. Also, remember many of the ship's copy machines use A4 (international-size) paper, so if you need to make copies bring the correct size paper.

Make your port letters personal. Use words like "you" and "yours" to include your readers in whatever you are writing about. Sign each letter and, again, include your company name and your cabin number.

Thank-You Letters

A nice ending to your clients' cruise experience is a note from you thanking them for traveling with you. These letters can be distributed the last night on board so they have them in their cabins first thing in the morning. Alternatively, you can mail them to their homes. (Be sure to get permission from your tour operator before contacting clients at their home address.) These letters should be personalized and prepared at the end of the cruise when you will have gotten to know your passengers individually.

Don't forget a thank-you letter to the on-board staff, thanking them for all their help and for any special arrangements or considerations they gave you. This gesture will be most beneficial the next time you bring a group on board.

Maps

Your clients will appreciate receiving maps. Maps give them a sense of security as well as a better mental picture of the area in which they are traveling. The ships do not always provide maps, and when they do, supplies are often limited.

City or Local Maps

Obtain a good detailed map of the port city (*Example 4.5*) from a tourist bureau. Highlight where the ship will dock. People always like to know the dock location, especially if they are sightseeing on their own. Continue highlighting all the sightseeing attractions mentioned in the ship's excursion booklet. If you have trouble pinpointing the attractions on the map, ask the shore excursions staff after you board. The staff will also be able to show you where the ship will dock.

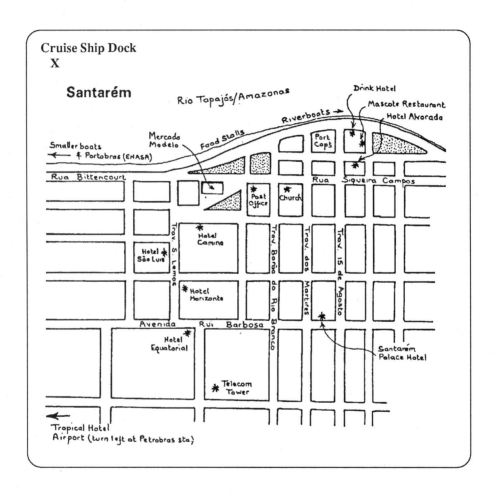

Example 4.5 Map of Santarem

Country Maps

On a map of the country (*Example 4.6*), highlight the cities you will be visiting. Highlight the port city where you will be docking and any other cities to which your excursions will take you. The map used in *Example 4.6* was created using a computer program called "MapArt," described under Resources (chapter 1).

South America

Example 4.6 Map of South America

Customs Information

You may want to provide your clients with a U.S. customs brochure called *Know Before You Go*. It explains all the details, restrictions and allowances passengers must comply with. Pick up brochures from the airport or ask a local customs office to send them to you. If you are not able to obtain enough brochures for everyone in your group, type the information for distribution. But don't make yourself a customs expert. If you are not sure of a regulation, ask an official U.S. customs agent. (And remember — shopkeepers in foreign countries are not customs experts.)

Record of Purchases

Clients really appreciate this handout *(Example 4.7)*, which allows them to record their purchases in foreign countries. As you can see, the form has a place for:

- ⚓ Date
- ⚓ Location (country)
- ⚓ Articles purchased
- ⚓ Cost in foreign currency
- ⚓ Cost in U.S. currency

Explain to clients that if they fill out the form as they go along, going through customs will be much easier. First, the customs people will think your clients more honest if they have listed everything and are organized. More important, if they are traveling in GSP (Generalized System of Preference) countries and have listed purchases by country, the customs people can easily deduct those items from customs allowances. Passengers can bring back products from GSP countries duty-free; that is, they will not be considered part of the customs declaration allowance of $400 per person. (GSP was established in 1976 to help developing countries improve their economies through exports.) Check with your local customs office to find out whether the countries you will be traveling in have GSP status.

Currency Conversion Chart

People on vacation love to buy souvenirs! On most cruises — especially during a shore excursion — there is not a lot of time to shop. The currency conversion chart *(Example 4.8)* will give your clients a quick idea of what items cost in foreign currency. This handout is a client favorite.

RECORD OF PURCHASES OUTSIDE U.S.

DATE	LOCATION	ARTICLE	COST/FOREIGN	COST/U.S.

Example 4.7 Record of Purchases

Notice the box "Compliments of" on the conversion chart. Be sure to fill it in; you want anyone who picks up this document to know you provided it.

Germany	Currency is the German Mark - rate as of (date)				
	There are $1.502 German Marks to 1$ US				
US$	GERMAN	US$	GERMAN	US$	GERMAN
1	1.50	41	62	475	713
2	3.00	42	63	500	750
3	4.50	43	65	525	788
4	6.00	44	66	550	825
5	7.50	45	68	600	900
6	9.00	46	69	650	975
7	10.50	47	71	700	1050
8	12.00	48	72	750	1125
9	13.50	49	74	800	1200
10	15.00	50	75	850	1275
11	16.50	55	83	900	1350
12	18.00	60	90	950	1425
13	19.50	65	98	1000	1500
14	21.00	70	105	1250	1875
15	22.50	75	113	1500	2250
16	24.00	80	120	1750	2625
17	25.50	85	128	2000	3000
18	27.00	90	135	2250	3375
19	28.50	95	143	2500	3750
20	30.00	100	150	2750	4125
21	31.50	110	165	3000	4500
22	33.00	120	180	3500	5250
23	34.50	130	195	4000	6000
24	36.00	140	210	4500	6750
25	37.50	150	225	5000	7500
26	39.00	160	240	6000	9000
27	40.50	170	255	7000	10500
28	42.00	180	270	8000	12000
29	43.50	190	285	9000	13500
30	45.00	200	300	10000	15000
31	46.50	225	338		
32	48.00	250	375		
33	49.50	275	413		
34	51.00	300	450		
35	52.50	325	488	COMPLIMENTS OF	
36	54.00	350	525		
37	55.50	375	563	Cruise Host Name	
38	57.00	400	600	Travel Time Tours	
39	58.50	425	638		
40	60.00	450	675		

Example 4.8 Currency Conversion Chart

This conversion chart was created with Excel, a computer spreadsheet program that allows you to create quick and accurate handouts for your clients. You simply input the foreign currency equivalent of one U.S. dollar and Excel does the rest.

Client Participation Activities
Name Bingo

Name bingo (*Example 4.9*) is a popular ship's activity and, because it requires passengers to collect names of others in the group, it's a great way to get people in your group to meet each other. Introduce it at a briefing or at the welcome cocktail party. After they have their cards filled with names (give them a time limit), place all the names in a bowl (cut up one of your rooming lists or write their names on slips of paper). Passengers check the names off their cards as each one is drawn, and the first one to cross off all the squares wins. Bring along a small prize for the winner.

Be sure to ask the ship's social staff or check the ship's newspaper before you try this game with your group. Remember, you don't want to duplicate or compete with the ship's activities.

Quizzes

Most ships have daily quizzes. Again, check with the ship's social staff to be sure they will not be distributing the same ones you have prepared.

Quizzes not only give your clients something to do while at sea, they are an excellent way for you to keep in touch with them. You might ask those in your group who want to participate to complete the quiz, note how long it took them, include their cabin number and return the quiz to your cabin. Give a small prize to the winners (more on prizes in chapter 9, Preparing for Special Occasions).

Here are some examples of quizzes you can prepare:

Currency Quiz:　When making up a currency quiz (*Example 4.10*) include currencies of the countries to which you will be traveling. Passengers match the correct currency with the country in which it is used.

Flag Quiz:　The flag quiz (*Example 4.11*) is another matching game. Again, be sure to include flags from the countries to which you will be traveling.

Travel Quiz:　Develop a list of travel-related questions (*Example 4.12*) referring to the specific city or country you are traveling to, or a variety of destinations.

NAME BINGO
Travel Time Tours

		Your Name		

The players begin by writing their names in the center square. They then go to others in the group and ask people to write their names in each square until the card is full. The caller reads the names by pulling them from a hat. Each player crosses out the names called until a winner (as in bingo) is found.

Example 4.9 Name Bingo

Travel Time Tours
COUNTRY CURRENCIES

Match the country with its accepted currency.

1. ARGENTINA	a. Baht
2. BRITISH VIRGIN ISLANDS	b. Yuan
3. NORWAY	c. Zloty
4. VENEZUELA	d. Guilder
5. BULGARIA	e. Dinar
6. PERU	f. U.S. dollar
7. GERMANY	g. Peseta
8. UNITED KINGDOM	h. Cruzeiro
9. BELGIUM	i. Lira
10. NEPAL	j. Krone
11. ITALY	K. Austral
12. POLAND	l. Mark
13. HOLLAND	m. Rupee
14. BRAZIL	n. Pound
15. SPAIN	o. Inti
16. PEOPLE'S REPUBLIC OF CHINA	p. Riyal
17. ECUADOR	q. Lev
18. THAILAND	r. Bolivar
19. YUGOSLAVIA	s. Franc
20. SAUDI ARABIA	t. Sucre

Client Name   Cabin Number   _____

                                Time Completed _____

_____

Example 4.10 Currency Quiz

Travel Time Tours
FLAG QUIZ

You will find 20 representations of flags. Each is the distinctive emblem of a particular country. Can you name the country? Even though the color is not shown, the pattern itself is unmistakable. A list of countries follows. Fill in the name of the country under the flag.

Australia	Canada	Chili	Czechoslovakia
Iraq	Great Britain	Greece	Israel
Jamaica	Japan	Liberia	North Korea
Pakistan	Panama	USA	Switzerland
Turkey		Norway	Yugoslavia

FLAGS

Client Name _____   Cabin Number _____

Time Completed _____

Example 4.11 Match the Flags

TRAVEL QUIZ

What's your travel I.Q.? Try your hand at the following questions to find out.

1. What is the oldest capital in the U.S.?

2. Who said, "I knew I shoulda made a left at Albuquerque"?

3. What should you tip your cabin steward on a cruise?

4. Where do gray whales spend the winter?

5. Where do you find Red Stripe beer?

6. Where does "the surf meet the turf"?

7. Where can you ride the William Tell Express?

8. What world capital is partly in Europe and partly in Asia?

9. Where would you find the original Little Mermaid?

10. What Scandinavian country celebrates the Fourth of July?

11. What is the significance of the measurements 9 by 16 by 22 inches?

12. Where would you take the Lunatic Express?

13. What tire company publishes guides?

14. Where do you find Blue Mountain coffee?

15. What Scandinavian city is called The White City of the North?

16. Did the Spruce Goose fly? If so, how many times?

17. In what state in what country is the Barossa Valley located?

18. What is the most popular activity there?

19. Where in Canada might you be invited to attend a winter beach party?

20. What is the new dance craze from Brazil?

Client Name_____   Cabin Number _____
                                         Time Completed _____

Travel Time Tours

Example 4.12 Travel Quiz

Certificates

Cruising provides several occasions for presenting passengers with souvenir certificates. For example:

⚓ Crossing the Equator

⚓ First-Time Sailor

⚓ International Sailor

If you have a computer graphics or desktop publishing program you can easily design these certificates. If not, you can purchase pre-made certificates from a stationery supply store. The certificates in *Examples 4.13, 4.14,* and *4.15* are included in the *Cruise Hosting Computer Program* described in the appendix. Bring along a good supply of them and, either by hand or by computer, (prior to boarding the ship) fill in the names of your clients and all pertinent information about the cruise. Take along blank certificates in case you discover, for example, that one of your clients prefers to use a nickname you didn't know about earlier.

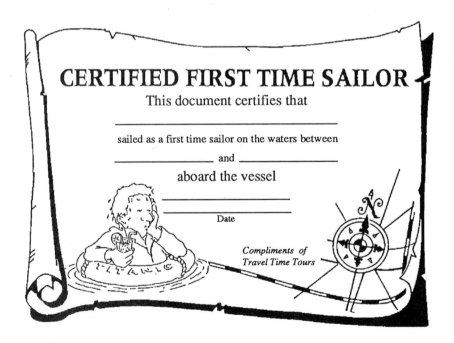

Example 4.13 First-Time Sailor Certificate

Example 4.14 International Sailor Certificate

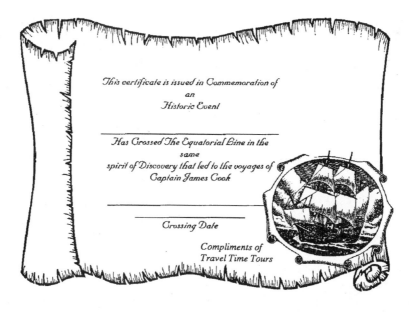

Example 4.15 Crossing-the-Equator Certificate

Deliver a crossing-the-equator certificate to clients' cabins on the day you actually cross the equator. The first-time sailor certificate, for passengers who are on their very first cruise, can be presented at a cocktail party or briefing. On any international cruise, certificates can be given to all clients at the end of the trip. You can use it as a gift at the farewell cocktail party or deliver the certificate to each cabin on the last day of the cruise. Make sure all certificates have some form of company identification on them. Otherwise, clients may think they came from the cruise line.

Miscellaneous Handouts

Various other handouts can be prepared to provide your people with information. Here's where you can have fun and be creative.

Heat Exhaustion: If you are traveling in a country that is close to the equator or is known for its hot climate, give instructions and tips on how your clients can protect themselves from the sun. Suggest they wear a hat, use sunscreen, carry a bottle of mineral water or take along a parasol. List the symptoms of heat exhaustion so they will recognize when they have it, although you really want them to know how to avoid it.

What Not to Pack: Depending on the country, security regulations and whether there is political unrest, there could be restrictions on luggage. Sometimes airports will require that you don't pack electrical appliances in checked baggage. They may also restrict batteries. These items will need to be packed in carry-on luggage. If you are aware of these restrictions, make a suggested packing list for your clients. This information could prevent them from being detained at the airport.

Nautical Terms: A list of nautical terms and definitions is particularly helpful for clients who have not sailed before. (See the glossary in the appendix.)

Pronunciation Guides: Although you have included a few foreign words and phrases in your port letters, prepare a longer list of the most commonly used words and phrases and their phonetic pronunciations for the country in which you are traveling (*Example 4.16*).

Final Disembarkation Notice: If you are very familiar with the ship and its final disembarkation procedures, this handout can be prepared prior to departure. This information is subject to change, however, so it may be wise to prepare this handout on board or, best, to hold a verbal briefing with your group giving them tips on what to do to get off the ship with the least amount of effort (see chapter 13, Final Disembarkation.)

Common Phrases In Spanish

Hola (ola)	Hello
Buenos Dias (Bwen-os deeas)	Good morning
Buenas Tardes (bwen-as tard-es)	Good afternoon
Buenas Noches (bwen-as no chays)	Good evening
Adios (ad-yos)	Goodbye
Hasta Luego (asta lweg-o)	See you later
Si (see)	Yes
No	No
Por favor (por fab-or)	Please
Gracias (grath-yas)	Thank you
De Nada (deh na da)	You're welcome
Perdone (pairdon-eh)	Excuse me
Lo Siento (lo se-ento)	I'm sorry
Habla usted ingles (able oosted in-gles)	Do you speak English?
No comprendo (no comprendo)	I don't understand
Comos esta usted (como-esta oosted)	How are you?
Muy Bien (mwee bee-en)	Very well
Como se llama (com-o seh yama)	What is your name?

DIRECTIONS

Donde esta la (dohn-day ehs-ta la)	Where is the
Para ir (para eer)	How do I get
al mercado (al maircad-o)	to the market
a la playa (ah la pla-ya)	to the beach
al puerto (al pwairto)	to the port
al centro de la ciudad (al thetro deh la thee-oodad)	to the town center
Donde estan los banos (Dohnday estan los bawn yos)	Where are the restrooms
Adelante (atalenta)	Straight on
un banco (oon banco)	a bank
una iglesia (oona eegles-ya)	a church
un restaurante (oon resta ooranteh)	a restaurant

COUNTING

Uno (oono)	One
Dos (dos)	Two
Tres (Trace)	Three
Cuatro (quatro)	Four
Cinco (sinko)	Five
Seis (sehs)	Six
Siete (see-eh teh)	Seven
Ocho (o-cho)	Eight
Nueve (new eh veh)	Nine
Diez (dee ehz)	Ten
Viente (vayn-tay)	Twenty

Compliments of (cruise host name) — Travel Time Tours

Example 4.16 Foreign Phrase Pronunciation Guide

Delivering Handouts

On most ships you will be able to slide your printed handout information under cabin doors. On the few ships where this won't work, you can roll up the papers and tuck them behind the door handle.

You can also ask the ship's staff (through the purser's office, steward's desk or housekeeping) to deliver your information. Although they will be willing to do it for you as a courtesy, it really is not their job — it is yours. When you deliver the handouts yourself you know that your clients actually received the information. Besides, it is a wonderful way to get your daily exercise!

You should deliver one set of materials to each couple and deliver a separate set for each single person sharing a cabin. Deliver your port letters and maps the afternoon before you arrive in each port. That way, your clients will have a chance to look them over before they go ashore.

This may seem like a lot of preparation. It is. But remember, you can do as much or as little as you want to. Of course, the more you do the better. Also, many of these documents need to be prepared only once (with occasional updates). Once you have done the initial preparation you can re-use documents on other cruises.

part II

ship ahoy

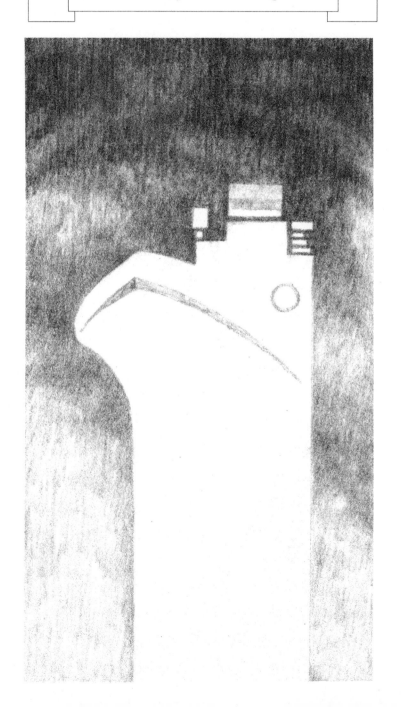

Chapter 5

Embarkation Day

So far, all we have talked about is the work — the preparation and research — that goes into a cruise. You may be a little overwhelmed at this point. Don't be. Once you start in, you'll find it all very satisfying, even fun. Here, on embarkation day, is where it all comes together. Chapters 5–14 will show you how all the work you have done frees you to enjoy yourself, your clients and the cruise.

Pre-Boarding

Plan to be on the ship two to three hours before your passengers board — two hours is the absolute minimum. Boarding before your passengers do is extremely useful and should be a priority concern. Your tour operator should have contacted the cruise line's sales office prior to the cruise and arranged for you to pre-board the ship. If this has not been done, getting permission to board early will challenge your social and negotiating skills. There are two major reasons why the ship may not allow early boarding:

- The cruise line wants to allow crew members enough time to ready the ship for arriving passengers. This job is best accomplished when no passengers are on board (and you are considered a passenger, not staff).

- Security is a prime concern for most cruise lines. Restricting those on board to known staff and crew makes their job simpler. Be thankful for such vigilance.

Remember, too, that many cruise lines are still unfamiliar with the duties of the professional cruise host, particularly since many cruise hosts are really tour operator staff taking free trips. They certainly don't perform the duties you are expected to as a professional cruise host.

Here are some suggestions to try to get yourself on board the ship before your clients arrive:

Arrange for Early Boarding Pass

- Ask your tour operator to prearrange with the cruise line's sales office for your early boarding pass. If this has been pre-arranged, the embarkation supervisor at the dock will then have your name on a list and all you will need to do is present identification.

- If your company is not willing to or can't arrange such a pass, call the cruise line's home sales office two weeks prior to the cruise. The cruise line itself will sometimes approve a pass for you. (Keep in mind that the tour operator you work for may not want you to contact the cruise line directly to request a pre-boarding pass. Consider this option carefully.)

When talking to the cruise line agent, tell them you are a professional cruise host and will be bringing a group on board. Give the ship, destination and sailing date. Mention that you have never been on the ship and need to orient yourself, deliver a welcome and information letter to your clients' cabins before they arrive, confirm cocktail parties with the cruise director and dining arrangements with the maitre d'. (Regardless of what the cruise line may say, most maitre d's want the cruise host to check with them before the passengers come on board). These are reasons enough to pre-board.

Most ships will give you some consideration. If you call and the cruise line does not cooperate, do not force the issue. Try the next approach.

Get Permission at the Dock

To receive permission at the dock to board early, you should arrive two to three hours prior to passenger embarkation. Ask to speak with the embarkation supervisor. Have your business card ready. (If your tour operator has not provided you with business cards, you should have had your own made. When supplying your own, simply state cruise host and your name, address and phone number.) Look and act like a professional. You may be able to explain your situation and talk your way onto the ship, depending on several factors:

- The mood of the embarkation supervisor at the time
- Whether the cruise line has a strict policy that no one is to pre-board without prior authorization from the home office
- The political unrest in the country of embarkation or in the world at the time

- How well you present yourself

- Good luck and timing!

If you fail, don't cause a scene. There is still hope! Continue on.

Get Permission at the Gangway

Check in with the other passengers and go to the waiting area. Scout around for people who are working in the boarding area. Look for the gangway supervisor (usually dressed in a police-type uniform). Here is where being a good judge of people comes in handy. This is my approach: With my business card in my hand and a big smile on my face, I approach the gangway supervisor and say, "I wonder if you could help me?" As I hand the guard my card I say, "I am bringing a group on board. I need to meet with the purser to check on guaranteed cabins and arrange for my briefing and cocktail party. Do you know the best way I could accomplish this?" I have, with one exception, been told, "Just follow the gangway. The purser's office is on the right."

Make a game out of trying to get on board. If you succeed, it will make your day. (But if you fail, don't let it ruin your day.)

Once on Board

The first and last days of a cruise are the busiest. They are known as turnaround days. Staff is saying good-bye to one group and welcoming another, all within a few hours. The staff is very busy with paperwork and they have a ship to clean, orders to place, food and cabins to prepare and meetings to attend.

Don't consume the staff's time on the first day. The staff does want you on board early to take care of business, but any business that can wait should wait until the following day. Even then, you must be flexible and wait for the people you need to see to become available. When you do see them, be prepared with your information or requests.

Having said that, the more arrangements you can make before your passengers board, the easier your first day will be. You may not be able to accomplish all of these tasks in the order they are presented here, but you should make every effort to do so. In any case, you *must* contact the purser's office, the maitre d' and the cruise director. Ideally, your first day will proceed as follows:

Find Your Cabin

Once on board, find your cabin and drop off your hand-carried luggage and paperwork. The very next thing you should do is to find and read the ship's newspaper so you will know the activities planned for the day. Check especially for the following information:

- When and where passengers meet with the maitre d' regarding dining room problems

- What meal service the ship provides, if any, before dinner

- When and where cruise staff introductions are made

- When and where the port talk is given on the day of embarkation (Port talks are always held the first evening if the ship is due in port the following morning.)

- Whether the mandatory lifeboat drill will be held on the first day and, if so, at what time. Locate your life vest – usually in the closet. If there is to be a drill, check the notice posted behind your cabin door to find the number and location of your muster station. When you are familiarizing yourself with the ship (see below) locate your muster station

Generally acquaint yourself with the first day's schedule of events. After you meet your clients they will ask you all these questions and more. (They often fail to read the information available in their cabin.) Keep a copy of the ship's newspaper with you at all times and suggest that your clients do the same.

Familiarize Yourself with the Ship

If you are not familiar with the ship, get your bearings. Go to all the decks and find the main function rooms. Passengers will ask you about the location of several places:

- Promenade deck (usually where the shops and entertainment are)

- Cocktail lounges / casino / disco

- Main showroom

- Dining room(s)

- Purser's office

- Doctor's office

- Movie theater

- Laundry facilities (if available)
- Public restrooms
- Pools / gym / massage / beauty salon

Meeting with Ship's Staff

The Purser: The purser's office is the main office on the ship. In fact, it is referred to as the "heartbeat" of the ship. It is here that you will go to get most of your questions answered or at least to be pointed in the right direction. Sometimes you can do your photocopying at the purser's office. For passengers, this is where all the finances are handled, bills paid, safety deposit boxes located, stamps purchased and letters mailed. If the ship has foreign money-exchange facilities, they will be available through this office.

Introduce yourself to the purser's staff (often you will work with the assistant purser). There are several things you need to accomplish here:

- Let the staff know you are a cruise host and give them your cabin number.
- Ask to see the berthing list or ship's manifest for your group to be sure the cabin numbers you have for your clients match those on the ship's list. (Sometimes the ship will upgrade a client after the documents go out and the cabin numbers will be different). Leave a copy of your passenger list with the purser's office.
- If you have any clients with guaranted cabins, obtain the cabin numbers for those clients. (A guarantee cabin is a cabin that was confirmed by the cruise line but a cabin number had not been assigned at the time your tour operator received documents from the cruise line.) You'll need this information before you deliver any prepared handouts.
- Ask the staff to advise you of problems, emergencies, cabin changes or last-minute cancellations pertaining to your group.
- Find out the ship's procedure for dispensing seasick pills. Do clients go to the doctor or can they be obtained from the cabin stewards or the purser's office? Is there a charge for the pills?

(Although you must connect with the purser's office the first day on board, the following can wait for several days.

Set up a master account on your credit card, requesting separate billings for your group and for your personal items. This master account is to cover such charges as:

- Your cocktail party (if not provided by the ship)
- Wine or gifts for birthdays and anniversaries
- Cocktails purchased for clients or cruise staff (if your company allows it)
- Small gifts for clients
- Group photos

The Maitre d':   (usually male) is a very important person on the ship. He can make or break your clients' dining experience. It is up to him to accommodate everyone's wishes for first and second seating, smoking and nonsmoking and table size (usually tables are set up for two to eight persons). This is an almost impossible task at best, but somehow the maitre d' manages to please most of the passengers. Your time with the maitre d' on the first day will be short, so have your paperwork organized when you sit down with him.

There are several things you will need to accomplish at your first meeting with the maitre d', and they are discussed in detail in chapter 10, Working With On-Board Staff. (If, as most maitre d's prefer, you can meet with him *before* passengers board, then be sure to review chapter 10 as part of your pre-boarding responsibilities.) Basically, you need to accomplish the following:

- Using the dining room seating request chart you developed earlier (*Example 3.2*), check your clients' seating arrangements and preferences. The maitre d' will go over them with you and try to ensure that clients get what they want. This is when the maitre d' gives you each client's seating request and table number. Client preferences cannot always be honored and, in that case, it will be up to your diplomacy skills to persuade clients that what they were given is quite all right.

- Give the maitre d' a copy of the birthday and anniversary list you prepared (*Example 3.4*). Confirm dates the events will be celebrated. Because these events are seldom celebrated the first day on board, arrange alternate dates for embarkation day celebrations. Confirm that a complimentary cake will be delivered to the table.

- If you don't already have one from a previous cruise, ask the maitre d' for a small diagram of the dining room (*Example 5.1*), showing the table layouts and table numbers. Later you can highlight the tables where your clients will be sitting so you'll know at a glance where they are located in the dining room. Some clients may be seated with passengers who are not on your tour. This is not the ideal situation but it's a typical occurrence, especially with large groups.

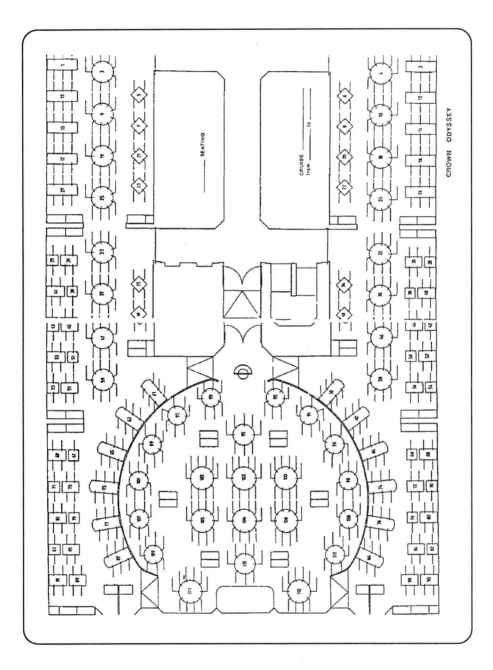

Example 5.1 Dining Room Diagram

Even though you may have met with the maitre d' earlier and have your table requests in hand, you should also be available at the scheduled time for passengers to make table or seating changes (you can find the time and place in the ship's newspaper). Passengers will line up for this purpose. Ask people in line whether they are from your group so that you can introduce yourself and find out what changes they want. Tell them that you will meet with the maitre d' to make the changes for them so that they won't have to wait in line. Once all the passengers have met with the maitre d', you should meet with him to discuss your required changes. When the change is made, offer to deliver a new table seating reservation card to your clients' cabins (otherwise the dining room staff will have to do it). The staff will greatly appreciate this gesture.

Some people will stand in line to meet with the maitre d' about their preference problems; others may wait in line just to see where their table is located. If they are there for table location only, you can take a burden off the dining room staff by helping your clients find their tables. This will also show the staff that you are there to be of assistance. In addition, the other passengers in line will quickly see that people who travel with your company are given VIP treatment. If your clients insist on waiting in line, however, talk with them about the ship or the cruise to take their mind off the wait.

Cruise Director: Briefings, office hours and sometimes cocktail parties are booked with the cruise director. (You need to know prior to boarding if the bar manager handles cocktail parties. A cruise host who has been on the ship before, your tour operator or the cruise line sales office should be able to tell you.) Contact the cruise director as soon as possible to set up briefing dates, times and places. Public meeting space and times are limited, especially if there are many groups on board. The cruise host who gets there first has the best choice of available rooms. Remember to bring your Cruise Data Sheet (*Example 3.10*) so that you can fill in times and dates for the ship's activities.

Bar Manager: If the bar manager books the cocktail parties, meet with him to confirm the times, places and dates. Discuss any food service, microphone requirements or availability of music. If your company has not provided invitations, ask the bar manager for the ship's generic invitations (*Example 3.7*).

Shore Excursion Manager: Try to contact the shore excursion manager to find out if a group buy is possible. Unless the ship will be in port on the first day of the cruise, the shore excursion manager will probably not be available. Again, leave a letter of introduction in their office, noting the number of passengers you have and asking whether a group buy is possible. Mention the date and time of your briefing and ask for a response prior to that time, if possible. (For more details on shore excursions and group buys, see Chapter 10, Working with the On-board Staff.)

Hospital Staff: Stop by the hospital or the doctor's office on the first or second day on-board ship. Give the staff a list of your passengers and their cabin number (a copy of your rooming list will do). Ask that someone let you know whether any of your clients visit the doctor. (You are required to fill out a report on each accident, injury or illness and sometimes your clients don't inform you that they are sick or injured.) It's very helpful to know the medical staff — you'll be working with them in times of emergency and for simple seasickness cases or minor injuries.

Contacting Unavailable Staff

Sometimes, the ship's staff you need to see will not be available. In these instances, deliver a note introducing yourself and stating the reason for the meeting (*Example 5.2*).

You can write these notes before getting on board, filling in the correct name once on board. By delivering them early you will get a jump on the other cruise hosts. It is very important that you specify desired times, dates and locations for your events, and that you offer to contact that staff person again. That way, you don't put full responsibility on the staff to chase after you. Be sure to print this letter on company stationary.

Completing Your First Day

Assuming you managed to board ahead of your clients, try to deliver all your handouts to their cabins so they will be there when your passengers walk in. Most of the time the cabins are unlocked and you can enter and place the materials on the bed or table. This is also ideal because it alerts you to such problems as a tender (ship-to-shore-boat) blocking a porthole view, for example. If the cabins are locked, simply slide the papers under the door or roll them up and tuck them behind the door handle. If you cannot accomplish this prior to passengers' boarding, it will afford you the opportunity to meet your clients in their cabins. The only drawback is that you may become engaged in long conversations, which will interfere with your delivery schedule.

Dear _____ (Use their name):

I am (your name) the cruise host with Travel Time Tours. I have arranged welcome and farewell cocktail parties for our group and I would like to meet with you, at your earliest convenience, to confirm a time and location for these functions. I have looked at the current ship's schedule and am familiar with the public rooms. Would the following times and locations be available?

| Welcome Cocktail Party | Disco | June 5 | 5:30 PM |
| Farewell Cocktail Party | Showroom | June 14 | 6:00 PM |

I am looking forward to meeting and working with you. Please contact me in cabin #A555, or I will stop by during your office hours tonight or tomorrow.

(Your name)
Travel Time Cruise Host

Example 5.2 Contacting On-Board Staff

Once all of these necessities have been handled, you may have time to do the following:

- Go to your cabin and unpack
- Get your life jacket for a lifeboat drill (if held the first day)
- Work on your dining room seating charts
- Tape a note pad and envelope to your cabin door so clients can contact you
- Walk around the ship and meet your passengers (hope that some will be wearing their name tags — if your company provides them)
- Put up client door decorations
- Go to dinner
- Be present at staff introduction (held on the first evening)

Dealing with Clients

You've met with the ship's personnel, now for your client group. Here are some questions frequently asked on the first day. Most answers can be found in the ship's daily newspaper (which you will have read).

- How should we dress for dinner tonight? (Dress is usually casual on the first and last nights of the cruise. See page 99 for dress details — what is considered casual, informal and formal.
- What time is dinner tonight?
- Is there any meal service before dinner?
- What time do the shore excursions leave tomorrow?
- Where are the various offices and social rooms?
- How do I mail a postcard?
- Where can I exchange money?
- Where is my suitcase?

These responsibilities all make for a very busy first day on board. Sometimes it is not possible to get everything done you would like. To a large extent you are dependent on how the cruise ship works and how much pre-boarding time you have. Every ship's itinerary and schedule is different. You will soon work out your own system. A lot of patience, organization and common sense on your part will come in handy. Just do all that you can and leave the rest for tomorrow. Enjoy your dinner, the rest of the evening — but be sure to be available to your clients.

Chapter 6

Holding Briefings

Briefings are group gatherings you hold to give your clients information they should have. There are several types of briefings. In this chapter we will discuss the initial briefing and the shore excursions briefing. The farewell party and final disembarkation briefing are discussed in chapter 13.

Initial Briefing

Your first (initial) briefing may be held on the day you board, especially if you will be in port early the following morning or for several days after boarding. You don't want to go too long before making contact with your group. Otherwise, they may feel that you are ignoring them. Mention that those who want to be on their own may certainly do so, but you'd love to have them participate. Remind them that you are there to add an extra level of service to their cruise experience.

Usually the initial briefing is held at about 9:00 A.M. on the first morning (after breakfast). Briefings should be a minimum of 30 minutes; 45 minutes to one hour is more typical.

Initial Briefing Procedures

Begin the initial briefing by telling your passengers a little bit about yourself. Your aim is to establish a friendly relationship as well as your credibility as a professional cruise host. Include such information as:

- Your name
- Where you live
- How long with your tour operator (unless it is your first trip)
- How long in the travel business (unless you are new)
- How many times on this ship and to these destinations (only if this is not your first time.)

The last three points raise a critical point that warrants discussion. It is the belief of most professional cruise hosts that they should be able to get on any ship and cruise any destination in the world without having previously done so. Nevertheless, the question every inexperienced cruise host dreads — "Have you ever taken this cruise before...and if so, how many times?" — does come up, and you must be ready to answer it. (Although it would be an asset to the cruise host to have a "familiarization cruise," perhaps as an assistant cruise host, it is often too expensive for the tour operator to provide this as a general practice.) There are some simple responses to these questions that work when the client is well-meaning and not trying to be "snippy." For example:

⚓ "You wouldn't believe me if I told you!"

⚓ "Not often enough."

⚓ "Not as many times as I would like to."

⚓ "Ask me that at the end of the cruise — after you've read all my handouts and sat in on my briefings."

Then change the subject.

If you think it's dishonest or unethical to tell the client anything less than the truth, please stop and think about it. Would you want to know you were the first patient to receive a heart bypass operation from your surgeon? How about your dentist telling you it's his first root canal? Most cruise passengers who have spent in excess of $10,000 per couple for a "dream vacation" do not want their bubble burst by inexperienced cruise hosts proclaiming enthusiastically that it's their first time!

Some cruise hosts make the false assumption that the clients will feel sorry for them if they confess to being new, and allow them more mistakes. Actually, the opposite happens. Clients are often angry and feel cheated. "Why don't we have a more experienced leader?" Whatever goes wrong, even when it is outside the cruise host's control, passengers tend to think: "If the cruise host had been more experienced, this would not have happened."

For what it's worth, you also have the backing of your company. In a survey of over 50 major tour operators across the United States, when asked whether their tour personnel should admit to first-time status on a ship or in a particular locale, their response was overwhelmingly "no."

The fact is that as a trained professional cruise host you have studied and researched for weeks before a cruise. If you've thoroughly reviewed this handbook, you will be more than ready for any ship or shore situation. And remember, you very likely know a great deal more than your passengers do. Even "veteran" travelers don't have your vantage point.

Although you probably know from questionnaires your tour operator sent whether your clients are seasoned or first-time travelers, ask the following questions to be sure the whole group feels included. These questions will also provide you with the information you need to determine how the rest of your briefing should proceed.

How many of you are cruising for the first time?   If there are a lot of first-time travelers you should gear this briefing more to them. You might introduce your remarks this way: "Many of you are familiar with what I'm going to say but let's go over it for the newcomers." Talk about things like:

- Shipboard life in general
- The ship's layout, facilities, activities
- Importance of ship's newspaper
- Dining room procedures and etiquette
- Nautical terms
- Tipping policy
- Shore excursions

Think of your own questions and concerns as a newcomer and add to this list.

How many of you have cruised on this ship?   Again, if you have a lot of first-timers, you must give a more detailed briefing on the ship's facilities and policies. (You see why familiarizing yourself with the ship is an important task.)

How many of you have cruised with this tour operator?   If many people raise their hands, it adds to your company's credibility and assures the ones who have *not* that they made a good choice. If only a few have, you may want to spend time explaining the special activities your company provides (cocktail parties, these kinds of briefings, etc), any forms your company requests clients to fill out (*Example 2.5* End-of-Cruise Evaluation) and why you were sent as a representative.

Suggested Topics for Initial Briefing

Here are some other topics to discuss at your first briefing. Choose the ones that pertain to your group's needs.

The Lifeboat Drill: If the ship has not held the mandatory lifeboat drill prior to your briefing, and especially if you have a lot of first-time cruisers, explain how this procedure works. Make sure they know that they are required to attend and that roll call *may* be taken. Tell them their life jackets are located in their cabins (usually in the closet but check your cabin to make sure) and their muster station number and location is noted on the back of the cabin door.

On-Board Purchases: Some ships require you to pay-as-you-go for drinks and other items purchased on board the ship. Most ships do not accept cash during the cruise. You simply sign for your purchases by name and cabin number and pay at the end of the cruise.

For ships that use this method of payment, there are four ways passengers can pay their accounts at the end of the cruise: credit card, cash, travelers' checks and, in some cases, personal checks. Advise clients to take their credit cards to the purser's office sometime during the cruise, and have their staff make an imprint of the card. (This is a very safe procedure. The cruise lines are totally honest and trustworthy. They have too much at stake to abuse credit card privileges.)

A day or so before the end of the cruise, clients will receive a review bill under their cabin doors. If there are any problems, they take the bill to the purser's office and ask the staff to make the necessary corrections. On the morning of disembarkation they will find a copy of their credit card receipts and a copy of their final bill under their cabin doors. There is nothing more they need to do.

Those paying by cash, travelers' checks or personal check need to stand in line at the purser's office on the last evening or last morning of the cruise to receive a copy of their bill, check it, and pay. Using a credit card is much more convenient — those lines can get long.

Air/Sea Envelopes: Explain that sometime during the cruise the ship's staff will hand out these envelopes and request that passengers submit all airline tickets to their final destination. Many people are reluctant to give up these tickets, so assure them that it is perfectly safe; the ship needs them to facilitate passengers' return flights.

Printed Handouts: Tell your passengers that you have assembled port information and maps for them, which you will be putting under their cabin doors throughout the cruise. Make sure they know you have provided and highlighted the maps yourself. (A recent survey of 500 clients showed that 84 percent thought these handouts were provided by the tour operator.) If you will be handing out Currency Conversion Charts (*Example 4.8*) and Record of Purchase Forms (*Example 4.7*) for customs, you might mention them specifically and explain how they work.

Shore Excursions: If you are not having a separate shore excursion briefing, explain the shore excursion program. Discuss the different ports of call and describe the essentials of the tour, climate, shopping, weather conditions and important (or amusing) local customs or laws. Let passengers know how to order and pay for these excursions, and how and when the tickets will be distributed. (See chapter 10 for more on shore excursions.)

Office Hours: Tell the group that you will be holding office hours on days the ship will not be in port. They can come to you with questions and concerns about destinations, other tours, shore excursions, grandchildren — anything. Alert them that you will deliver a printed notice to their cabins regarding time and place.

Clients' Responsibilities: If they are spending the day in port on their own, make sure they know it is their responsibility to get back to the ship before it sails. In case they miss the ship, they must get to the next port at their own expense. Instruct them to carry along a postcard of the ship or the ship's newspaper, which usually has the name of the port or port agent. If they get lost and don't know the language, either of those will aid them in getting back to the ship. When the next port is in a different country, however, they will need their passports, (or a photocopy of the front page with their photograph). They should also take credit cards or money when they go ashore. Make sure they fully understand that getting to the next port will be at their own expense.

Because the ship is required to show passports to get port clearance, some cruise lines retain all passports for the duration of the trip. Assist your clients by finding out what the ship's policy is here; ask the purser's office staff or passenger service representatives. If the ship has copying facilities, you can assist your clients by making copies of the first page of their passports. Then return the passports to the purser's office.

Standing in Line: Tell your clients that even though they will often have to line up for passports, baggage tags, or tender tickets, they don't have to be first in line! It may be hard to convince them. Tell them you know *from experience* if they wait awhile after the announcement, there will be little or no line. Let them know that the ship must bring together passengers and documents in time to get passengers where they need to be, and that if passengers have not picked up passports, or whatever, the ship will use the public address system to alert them.

Passenger Complaints: Tell your people to come to you, not to fellow passengers, if they have a complaint. Let them know that you are the only one (except for the cruise staff) who can help, and that if they don't tell you about a problem or concern in a timely fashion it could ruin their entire trip. If they insist on dealing with the staff, tell them that a big smile and an understanding attitude will get them a lot more than screaming or demanding.

Motion Sickness: There is always a chance that your ship will encounter rough water, and that some passengers will become seasick. Those who have the new Transderm-Scop ear patches for motion sickness should know that they sometimes cause a very dry mouth. Consuming more fluids (nonalcoholic!) or sucking on an ice cube is a good idea. (Let them know also, that if one patch is good, the idea that two must be better is definitely false — in fact, the opposite is true.) Some passengers may be wearing a product called Sea-Bands or AcuBands which apply pressure at the "Nei-Kuan" accupressure point on the wrist and thereby prevent or quell seasickness.

Some other preventive ideas for seasickness that you can suggest are:

- When walking, take lots of little steps instead of big steps. It helps minimize the rolling motion sensation that makes you queasy.

- Stay on the open deck instead of inside the cabin.

- Don't lie down; do something, keep moving.

- No matter what, *don't* drink alcoholic beverages or acidic juices (like orange juice). *Do* try to consume something: toast, crackers, rice, bread, applesauce, oatmeal, hot tea.

- Taking ginger pills (obtained in health food stores) works for some people. I have used them effectively. Remember, however, as a cruise host you cannot diagnose or recommend medications.

If preventive methods fail and your clients succumb, direct them to the medical staff for a shot, which works right away. (The doctor will charge a fee for this service.) Also advise them on how to obtain seasickness pills from the ship's staff and whether there is a charge for this medication.

Party Protocol: When you tell your passengers about the cocktail parties (welcome and farewell), it is very important to let them know that nonalcoholic beverages will also be available. You want nondrinkers to feel welcome; sometimes they feel uncomfortable about attending something called a "cocktail party" when they don't drink. For that reason, in fact, you may want to call your party a *welcome reception*, a *farewell party*, or a *bon voyage party* instead of a cocktail party.

Gratuities: Tipping is an important part of any cruise. Ships have different policies regarding how their staff is paid. Some ships have a blanket no-tipping policy. Most ships do have a tipping policy and will discuss it with passengers during the disembarkation talk or at a special end-of-cruise talk. Notes on tipping are also published in the daily ship's newspaper toward the end of the cruise. Some ships require that all tips be pooled and the waiters, cabin stewards, deck help and busboys share in them equally. Some allow waiters, busboys and cabin stewards to keep their individual tips. (You and your clients might be interested to know that some ships require their waiters and cabin stewards to turn in their tips in the amount already conveyed to passengers. If they are tipped *less*, they have to make up the difference. If they are tipped more can they keep the difference.)

In general, you can expect to tip bar waiters and wine stewards as you go along for bar drinks (including sodas which are not part of the cruise package.) But, no matter how it is done, remind your group that these people make very small salaries and tips are a very important part of their income.

If your company has a *prepaid* tipping policy (all gratuities for on-board staff included in the price of the cruise), reassure the clients that you will be taking care of the gratuities for the maitre d', head waiters, waiters, busboys and cabin stewards. But let them know that additional gratuities are always welcome for special service "beyond the call of duty."

Dining Room Courtesies: Meals are one of the most important features of the cruise experience. Familiarizing your people with the dining room staff and their responsibilities will help to ensure that everyone involved goes away happy! Here are the key people and their functions:

- The maitre d', usually with an assistant, oversees the entire dining room.
- The head waiter is responsible for special orders, special food preparation at the table, and the management of his or her section of the dining room, including supervising waiters and busboys for their section. (Clients with special food requests should talk with their head waiter.)
- The wine steward serves the wine at meals or arranges for drinks from the bar. Wine ordered with dinner does not have to be finished at one meal. The wine steward can recork the bottle and serve it the next day for lunch or dinner. Passengers who receive wine in their cabins can have the cabin steward send the wine to the dining room to be served at their next meal. (Incidentally, clients are not allowed to bring wine to the dining room that has been brought from home or purchased in port or at duty-free shops.)
- A waiter takes orders for meals.
- The busboy serves water and bread, helps serve the main meal and generally keeps dishes cleared from the table.

Some special considerations apply to dining room protocol and mealtimes. Alert your group to the following:

- It could take a day or two to effect changes in dining room seating. Ask them to be patient.

- Although passengers do not have to sit in the same seat, they are required to remain at the same table throughout the cruise. It ensures better service: their waiters get to know them, what they like to eat and how they like it prepared. (On some nights there is open seating, meaning that between set hours passengers can eat in any dining room — if there is more than one — and at any table.

- It is customary to ask a table mate to notify the waiter when someone knows he or she can't be present at a meal.

- It is important to be on time for meals. The later passengers arrive, the later the waiters have to work. Dining room staff are up early in the morning to prepare for and serve breakfast; they then work lunch and dinner hour. They work very hard with very little time off during the cruise. Obviously they cannot ask a guest to leave the dining room. Suggest that clients be aware of the time and continue after-dinner conversations in a cocktail lounge.

- There are other meal options for breakfast and lunch. All ships serve buffets or offer food service at the pool or in another part of the ship. Room service is also available through the cabin steward.

- Those who are concerned about not getting back to the ship in time for a meal because of a long shore excursion should be reassured to know that, no matter what, no one has ever gone hungry on a cruise! If a shore excursion runs late, staff will hold the dining room open or will serve a buffet. They can even order a meal in their cabins. Furthermore, the ground operator who provides the shore excursions will include any meals that would otherwise be missed on the ship.

Dress Code: Give your clients suggestions on the proper dress while on board ship and in port. They will want to know how dressy the formal nights are. Ships vary. If you have not been on board before, ask the social staff — prior to your briefing — how dressy formal nights are. Clients want to know those occasions where they don't *have* to dress but can if they want to. Follow these general guidelines for on-board events:

	Men	**Women**
casual	slacks & shirt or polo shirt	shorts, slacks, skirt, dress
informal	suit or sportcoart & tie	cocktail dress, dressy dress, dressy slacks outfit
formal	dark suit & tie or tuxedo	cocktail dress or long evening gown

Bathing suits are never allowed in the dining room.

In port, dress will vary according to climate, local customs and religious attractions clients plan to visit. (You'll need a head covering for visiting the Vatican, for example.) Wear shorts and short-sleeved shirts for tropical climates, slacks and coats for glacier visits. Talk about precautions such as not wearing expensive jewelry, using sun protection, etc. More information about dress is covered in the shore excursion briefings section later in this chapter.

Evaluation Forms: If your tour operator supplies you with client end-of-cruise evaluation forms (*Example 2.5*) that you need to collect, let your clients know they will be coming. Tell them how important they are and that you are expected to return evaluations with your reports. Let them know that tour operators use this information for planning future cruises. Also let them know that the ship will be distributing its own end-of-cruise evaluation form for passengers to complete.

This is a good time to give your people general advice about filling out these evaluations. For example, they should be specific in their criticisms. If they had trouble with flights that were booked by the cruise line (as most are), they should not rate your company's service badly. Similarly, if the food was not to their liking, they should not rate their waiter poorly. When your company's evaluation form asks them to rate the cruise host, tell them it means you and not the ship's cruise director. They often get the two confused.

To assure that you get these evaluations back, let them know *now* to bring their completed forms in sealed envelopes to the farewell party where they will be rewarded with a drawing and a prize.

Shipboard Credit: If your tour operator has contracted with the cruise line for your clients to have shipboard credit, make sure clients know any limitations imposed — only the boutique and bar or including shore excursions and beauty salon, for example. Make sure they know that this credit must be used while on board the ship — that is, no credit will be issued for unused portions after they return home. If there are two single people in one cabin, suggest they keep their charges separate to qualify for this credit.

Flight Concerns: Clients who experienced problems with the departure flights the cruise line arranged are likely to be concerned about their return reservations. If you know that many passengers had problems, you may want to mention it in your briefing. Tell them that you know they have concerns but that you cannot get answers from the staff until the middle or towards the end of the cruise. For your part, however, you should approach the staff two to three days into the cruise. If the problem is one of seating, the staff must be made aware of it at the time they are assigning seats for the return flight. After seating has been completed, it is difficult for the staff to take care of special requests.

Never bring up problems (such as late documents or bad flights) unless they relate to the entire group. If clients bring up individual problems, tell them you will be happy to talk with them privately so as not to take up the group's time. Suggest they see you during office hours or after the briefing.

Final Disembarkation: Talk briefly about final disembarkation procedures for the return flight: if the ship collects airline tickets, discuss the air/sea envelopes (*Example 13.2*) and how seating is done (by the ship or the airline). Tell clients to attend the ship's disembarkation talk as well as your own briefing on the subject. If you let them know they will hear more later, they may worry less during the cruise, especially if they have had previous problems. (More about end-of-cruise briefings in chapter 13, Final Disembarkation.)

Client-initiated Changes: Explain to your group the importance of notifying you if they change cabins or dining room tables on their own. You often have important information you need to get to them, and the ship will not automatically notify you of changes.

One couple approached me five days into the cruise, for example, and told me that I owed them a drink. When I inquired why, they told me that they never received an invitation to the welcome cocktail party. I looked at my check-off list. I had their cabin number checked off so I knew I had delivered the invitation (another reason for delivering your own information and keeping good records). When I showed them I had checked off their cabin number, they told me they had changed their cabin the day after boarding. Neither they nor the ship's staff notified me.

Emergency Information: If your tour operator required clients to fill out confidential client information sheets and you do not have all of them, ask that they give them to you as soon as possible. The emergency information is very important in case of accident or medical problems. Make sure they understand the urgency of this information as some may be reluctant to give it. However, if clients refuse to provide you with this form, you cannot force them.

Names and Faces: Some clients don't like wearing name badges and some companies don't even provide them. Although it is not that hard to learn names and faces, ask clients to say hello and tell you their names if they see you don't recognize them. Develop your own special way of telling them that they have to know only one of you but you have to recognize 50 or 150 of them.

Ship's Amenities: Discuss any special amenities the ship offers, such as the free laundry (if available), exercise and gym facilities, Jacuzzis and saunas.

Doubling up Briefings: Depending on how much time you have at your initial briefing, you may want to include with it a shore excursion briefing. If time is short, however, you can schedule this briefing for later. In any case, discuss the ship's embarkation card (*Example 6.1*), an identification card issued to each passenger. Passengers must take their cards each time they leave the ship. They will be required to show their cards to the security officer before re-boarding at every port.

CRUISE CARD

Stateroom ID		Voyage	
A438	**01**	**4711**	**17 Mar**
Embarkation		Debarkation	
San Juan		**Acapulco**	
Name			
Smith	**A**		
Signature			

Example 6.1 Embarkation Card

Facilitating Contact: Let your people know that you will have a note pad and envelope on your cabin door so that they can leave you a message when you're not there. Some prefer this to seeing you at office hours. (See Chapter 7, Maintaining Contact with Your Group.)

Door Decorations: If you use cabin door decorations (described in chapter 3), explain that they make it easier for you to find cabins when you deliver information. Even with that, don't be surprised if some people remove them.

Participation in Ship's Activities

Once you know the various events the ship has planned for its passengers, do what you can to encourage your clients to join in.

Fashion Shows: Sometimes the boutique will have a fashion show on board and will use passengers as models. Before your briefing, check with the boutique. (If you are still in port, the boutique, by law, will be closed; you can ask the social staff.) They don't have to be a professional model, of course, and these fashion shows are lots of fun. Participants usually receive a gift or small discount from the boutique for their willingness to model.

Dance Lessons: Encourage your group (especially unaccompanied single passengers) to take advantage of the dance lessons — even if they know how to dance. If you have a lot of singles, tell them you will meet them there. (Then you can introduce them to other singles. I have found that people I've introduced became friends and dance partners for the entire cruise.)

Singles and Male Cruise Hosts (escorts):   You may find yourself traveling with many single seniors, mostly women. Because of this trend, some ships hire men to talk to, dance with and entertain single women. Introduce these male cruise hosts to your single women or point out your singles to the escorts so they can ask your clients to dance. Let your single women know that these hosts are there for them. If they want to dance it is very appropriate to approach a male cruise host and ask him.

Passengers with Children: Depending on the itinerary and time of year, you may have clients who bring their children. Treat them as part of the group, including them in the various events you hold.

Many ships have youth counselors who provide daily activities for the kids, even taking them on special shore excursions. Make sure the parents know about these activities. Do not, however, become a baby sitter. That is not your responsibility. Parents can obtain baby-sitting services from the ship's staff. Do not offer to take the children off the ship on shore excursions. You and your tour operator would be held liable if anything happened.

Book and Magazine Swap: Mention that toward the middle of the cruise you will arrange for people to exchange reading materials. (See chapter 8, Hosting Group Activities.)

Shore Excursion Briefings

If you have time and if you are familiar with the area, this briefing is a great service to provide to your clients. Make suggestions about the tours you believe will be best for their abilities and interests. (Here is when you can make good use of your confidential client information sheets and the resource material you assembled.) It may be best, especially if your briefing times are limited, to give your clients an overview of all the tours. Then, encourage them to go to the individual port lectures and shore excursion briefings held by the ship's staff before making their final decisions.

Ship's staff have been known to discourage passengers from taking tours. For example, in South America, one ship's cruise director discouraged all the passengers from taking the ten-hour river cruise, jungle walk and evening alligator hunt. He said that the walking was too hard and that none of the passengers were in good enough physical condition for the tour. The real reason was that the cruise director was tired of passengers complaining about the heat and humidity characteristic of the region. Because I had been on that excursion, I knew the walking was not that difficult and that they would have a great time. I was able to describe the tour in detail and felt that those who wanted to participate met the level of fitness required. The people who had their hearts set on going went, and were thrilled to have had the experience.

To get your group excited about shore excursions, use this briefing time to tell them:

The Highlights of What They Will See: Before your briefing, highlight the attractions in your shore excursion book and, if you are familiar with the attractions, go into detail when you speak. Paint colorful, vivid pictures from your own experience (or from your reading materials, if you know they are reliable.)

The Length of the Tour and the Weather: A seven-hour bus tour in humid weather can be difficult, especially if you're not prepared for it or if you are elderly. So prepare your group ahead of time.

Special Tips: This is the time to use the information you researched when preparing your shore excursion briefing materials. You can pass on tips about:

- Transportation — Some tours use old school buses with no air conditioning.

- Conveniences — Most coaches in foreign countries do not have rest rooms; some tours do not take frequent restroom or beverage stops. Suggest that your clients take bottled water when leaving the ship.

- Language problems — Some countries use local guides who do not speak English very well.

Dressing for Shore Excursions: Mention, for example, not wearing shorts if the shore excursion includes a temple visit (when legs must be covered) or not wearing jewelry in poverty areas or in cities like Rio de Janeiro where crime can be a problem.

Which Tours to Take: From your experience (if you are familiar with the tours) you'll know which are the better value for the money and the most appropriate for your clients' abilities. Again, judgment is crucial. You need to have talked with your clients to know their interests and desires. Try not to let your personal likes and dislikes play a part in your tour suggestions.

Taxi Services: Before arriving in port, find out who may want taxis so you can arrange ride-sharing for private touring.

Meeting Together after the Excursion: Pick a spot on the ship — a lounge that has happy hour or hors d' oeuvres, for example — where those who went on excursions can meet to share their experiences with you and the rest of the group. These sessions will provide you with valuable first-hand information about the tours, which you can use for future cruises.

Group Buys: If the shore excursion office allows you to do a group buy, i.e., to order all the shore excursion tickets for your group, explain how it works. Group buys must be prearranged, but it saves your passengers the trouble of waiting in line to purchase tickets. (For more information see chapter 10, Working with the On-Board Staff.)

Disembarkation Policy for Excursions: Explain the ship's disembarkation policy for shore excursions. Find out this information in advance by asking the shore excursion manager. Sometimes passengers disembark according to deck, sometimes just by tour number or tour time. Remind clients to take their embarkation cards (*Example 6.1*). Due to security, they cannot re-board without them.

Reserved Motorcoach: Although not the norm, some ships, depending on the size of your group and the country you are traveling in, allow you to use a separate motorcoach for your passengers. If you have arranged a coach for your group, be sure to tell your passengers where to meet so you can all board the coach together.

"Humorous" Questions: Be prepared to hear some questions and remarks for which there may be no real answer. For instance:

- "Should I go to the bathroom *before* we leave the ship?"

- "Do I have to go to the shore to pick up the tour?"

- Sometimes shore excursion passengers disembark by deck. One lady asked, "If I don't get off when my deck is called do I have to stay on the ship?"

- One cruise host told her people she would meet them on the pier. A lady called her at 5:00 A.M. and said, "I have been looking at the ship's diagram all night and I can't find the pier!"

- During a shore excursion talk on an Alaska cruise, the discussion was about the millions of barrels of oil that are pumped through the pipeline from Prudhoe Bay to Valdez every day. One client asked, "What do they do with all the barrels once they get to Valdez; ship them back?"

You quickly learn that part of the skill of a good professional cruise host is to respond kindly and appropriately to these "unusual" questions.

Dealing with No-Shows

It is important that you know whether or not your clients have attended your briefings and cocktail parties (especially your initial briefing) because if they have not, you must arrange to give them your information and handouts individually. The best way to track attendance and determine your no-shows is to use your rooming list. When clients come to the briefing ask for their cabin numbers. (As mentioned earlier, asking for a cabin number is less offensive than asking their names, which they may expect you to know at this point.) Cross off the cabin numbers as you get them; the ones not crossed off are no-shows.

Contact your no-shows as soon as possible after the initial briefing or party. You want to find out whether there is a problem or whether they just don't want to be part of the group. (Otherwise they may write on the post-cruise evaluation form that you ignored them.) There are different ways to do this:

- Call them and say, "Sorry we missed you at the briefing (or cocktail party.") Pause, leaving it open for them to say, "We are too, but we wanted to take a shower (or a nap)," or "We won't be joining in the group activities but thank you for calling," or whatever reason they have.
- Write notes to your no-shows and put them under their cabin doors. Tell them you missed them at the party or briefing and you hope everything is okay.

If they missed a briefing, include in your note a short description of the main points that were covered.

Chapter 7

Maintaining Contact with Your Group

One of the hardest things to do is to stay in contact with your group members throughout the cruise. Because it is almost your most important responsibility, let's recap some of the ways the cruise host remains visible to the clients.

Office Hours

Holding office hours each day you are at sea is a good opportunity for your clients to talk with you. They may have concerns or problems, or they may want to talk about future tours and destinations.

As stated earlier, before arranging your office hours, contact the cruise director or purser's office for a time and place that doesn't conflict with the ship's activities. And *never* book anything during bingo!

Some ships will give you an area and set up a table for you. On other ships you simply pick a lounge or other public area. Just be sure it is a place where your clients can easily find you. While you wait for clients to come to you, you can use the time to write cocktail party invitations or take care of other paperwork, such as reports to your company.

Be prepared for humorous questions like, "What elevation is the ship at now?" "What time is the midnight buffet?" "Does the crew sleep on board?" and "Does the ship have its own electrical power?"

Dinner Time

A good way to keep in touch is to do table rounds at dinner. You will have already prepared your group dining request form (*Example 3.3*) and your dining room diagram (*Example 5.1*) so you will know where everyone is sitting.

Table rounds work well as a way to stay in touch with your group, but don't do them every night. If you are on an 18-day cruise, your clients will be dreading seeing you after about the fifth night! Do them only when there has been little or no contact with your group that day. (You might do them also on shore excursion days to make sure everyone returned!)

Skip table rounds on formal nights, especially if you attended the captain's cocktail parties and talked with your clients there. If you must do rounds on these special nights, keep them short and simple.

When doing table rounds you must stay out of the waiters' way. They have a job to do and little space in which to do it. If you let the waiters know that you are concerned about staying out of their way, joke with them and smile a lot, your rounds will be well accepted.

Visit each table where you have clients and say hello. Ask them how their day was or tell them something special they need to know for the following day. Keep conversations short. Remember that the other passengers at the table (who are not with your group) won't want to be disturbed by announcements that pertain only to your functions. Incidentally, when doing table rounds the first night, do them later in the meal, not at the beginning. It's better to give your clients a chance to get to know their table mates.

For example, on the first night, don't ask clients whether they are happy with their tables. Once, at the beginning of the meal I asked that question of two single senior ladies. They were at a table of eight and the others at their table were married couples. At my inquiry, they began to insist on moving. Eager to assure my clients' happiness, I went immediately to the maitre d' and explained the situation. He changed their table for the following night. When I returned to the women to tell them the good news, they were well into conversations with the couples at the table and no longer wanted to move! Give your people time to settle in before raising possible problems.

Just as you may not have all your people at one table, you won't always have them at one seating. Obviously, when you are not yourself scheduled to eat, you have ample time to visit your clients at their tables. When you are eating your own meal and having to do table rounds, then it is important to order your food *first*, do rounds, and be back at your table when soups and salads are being served. The waiters work on a tight schedule and you don't want to interfere with the flow of service nor disrupt the meal for your table mates.

If you have a small group (15-25 people) and they are all seated together with no other cruise passengers, you may want to sit with your group. If you do this, it's best you keep the same seat for dinner and then move to another table for dessert. Set up your personal dining preference with the maitre d' at your initial meeting. (In most cases you will want to be seated with other cruise hosts or cruise passengers.) Remember, if you can't sit with all of your clients, you should not sit with any of them.

Outside the Dining Room

Simply standing outside the dining room and being available as passengers come in to dinner is a good alternative on nights that you don't do table rounds. It also works on ships where space is very limited and dining rooms are not set up for table rounds.

Miscellaneous Contact
Port Letters, Parties and Private Tours

All of the efforts you make via letters, parties and private tours are also excellent ways of making yourself known and remembered. See chapters 4 and 8 for detailed discussions of these miscellaneous contacts.

On-Board Photographers

Throughout the cruise photographers are everywhere snapping photos of passengers. Photos are mounted on a wall in a specifically designated area where passengers can view them (and buy prints, of course). Make a point of looking at the photographs; if you see a particularly good photo of one of your clients, tell them about it. That you remembered them, and took time to comment, will make them feel special.

Photos from the Tour Operator

Confidential client information forms sent to you by your tour operator may have client photographs attached. Return these photos to your clients near the end of the cruise or after you are sure you know their faces and names. Slide them under their cabin doors with little notes or give them back in person. The clients will appreciate this gesture.

On the Dock

When you are not accompanying a shore excursion, being on the dock to see your passengers off is a good way to be visible. You must walk a fine line between helping your clients and staying out of the way of the shore excursion staff. Understand your role. (Chapter 10, Working with On-Board Staff, discusses your role during shore excursions.)

Cabin Door Communications

As suggested, the first day of the cruise is when you should tape a large decorative envelope (obtained from a stationery or drug store) to your cabin door with a pad and pen attached (*Example 7.1*). It is a sure way for clients to get messages to you and it is also convenient for them — they won't have to disturb you at all hours. You may even get some interesting messages from other cruise passengers (or crew) that will make your day! (Like "Meet me at the bar at 4 P.M., Joe from California.") Be sure to include some form of company identification.

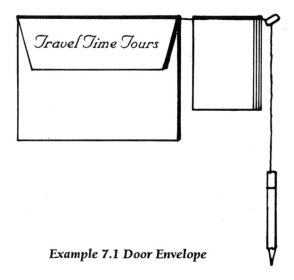

Travel Time Tours

Example 7.1 Door Envelope

Dealing with Large Groups
Large Groups with More Than One Cruise Host

If you are traveling with a large group (60 to 200 or more passengers) and more than one cruise host has been assigned to escort the group, some special rules apply. Before boarding, go over them with her or him to be sure you are clear about your individual and joint responsibilities.

- Treat the group as one. Never split passengers up into smaller groups as a way to share responsibilities between you.

- Do split office-hour duties, however. One cruise host can hold office hours in the morning and the other in the evening. With larger groups you may need to hold office hours twice a day.

- Both cruise hosts should be present for all group activities such as cocktail parties, briefings and other planned group events.

- Hold all functions as one large group function; you want all the passengers to feel they have been treated equally.

- Rotate your nights for table rounds so all the passengers get to deal with both of you. Avoid having both of you visit a table on any given night — just be sure all clients are greeted by both cruise hosts during the cruise.

- Switch off or divide equally the task of delivering port information or decorating doors.

- At the end of the cruise, both cruise hosts should share gratuities equally.

When there are two cruise hosts of the same sex assigned to a large group, the tour operator usually arranges for them to share a cabin.

Chapter 8

Hosting Group Activities

As noted at the outset, some people wonder what cruise hosts can possibly do for their clients that the cruise staff doesn't already do. A creative cruise host will think of all kinds of activities to assure that the group in his or her care has the best trip possible. The possibilities are limited only by time. Just remember — *never* schedule a function at an hour that conflicts with one of the ship's major activities! Again, read the ship's newspaper carefully. Below I will talk about activities you as cruise host conduct and events put on by the ship's staff.

Activities You Conduct
Cocktail Party Preparation

As mentioned earlier, the tour operator, the cruise line or both may provide a cocktail party for your group. If it is a long cruise and the group is large enough, you usually have a welcome party and a farewell party, one provided by the cruise line (complimentary) and the other paid for by your tour operator. Regardless of whether the cocktail party is sponsored by the cruise line or the tour operator, you will be the host, and it is up to you to make them festive.

If you have clients at both seatings in the dining room, the best time to hold a cocktail party is 45 minutes prior to the first seating for dinner.

- The day before the event, send invitations to: the captain, purser, cruise director and assistant cruise director, social hostess, shore excursion staff, passenger service representatives and other staff, as appropriate (e.g., male cruise hosts as escorts, entertainers) as well as your passengers.

- On the day of the party, go to the party room you've reserved and introduce yourself to the bartender and waiters. This is a good way to ensure good service. Whether or not you plan to decorate, be there 15 to 20 minutes early to make sure tables and chairs are set the way you want them. (In addition, some clients always come early and may be there when you arrive.) Make sure you have a working microphone (if you requested one). If you are sharing a main lounge with other groups, the ship may not allow you to use a microphone.

- Check on any food and beverage service you requested. If you have prepared handouts for your clients, assemble them in a convenient place for distribution — but remember, if they are on their way to dinner or other ship's activity directly following your party, they may not want to carry papers with them or they might forget to look them over carefully. (In this case, deliver the handouts to clients' cabins.)

- Decorate the party room with balloons. Put long strings of ribbon on them and curl or shred the ends. Tape them to the ceiling, walls and posts around the room. Some cruise hosts put balloons on the tables and encourage people to blow them up and toss them back and forth. Whether or not you do this depends on your group and your personal style. Hang streamers around the room. It is not the ship's responsibility to provide decorations. If you don't have enough balloons and streamers, however, the social staff may be willing to give you some. And remember, if you put up decorations, be sure to take them down after the party. Always leave the room as you found it. You don't want to create extra work for the ship's staff.

- Assuming you arranged to have musicians, check with the bar manager to reconfirm.

Cocktail Party Activities

Depending on the time of the cocktail party (and it will always vary), and the size of your group, here are some ideas that have worked for me:

- For an icebreaker, as each person enters the room give him or her a slip of paper with the name of someone in the group on it. Ask the client to find the other person and introduce him- or herself. This "forces" people to meet others in their group. The first reaction will be, "But I don't know who that person is!" If you just smile in response, they quickly understand the concept. This idea has never failed. If there is a holiday during the cruise, write the passengers' names on holiday decorations — a red heart for a Valentine's Day or a shamrock for St. Patrick's Day. If you don't like your handwriting, just cut up a rooming list on which the names are already typed. Remember that name bingo (*Example 4.9*) is also a good icebreaker.

- Have guests stand up, one by one, and introduce themselves, including their occupation and where they live. (This works best with small groups.)

- With larger groups, call out state names and ask passengers to stand when their state name is called. (Read your information sheets to recall which states are represented.) This way other people can see who is from their area. Or put up signs around the room with state names on them. Ask clients to gather by their state sign as they enter.

- Call out different hobbies (for example, golf, bridge, backgammon, shuffleboard, knitting, collecting antiques) and ask people with those hobbies to stand. This way, people interested in playing bridge, shuffleboard, or ping pong can find partners, or those with similar hobbies can share conversations.

- Set up astrological signs around the room and, as guests enter, ask them to gather under their sign. This not only breaks the ice but you get to find out who might be having a birthday while on the cruise. (But, never ask the group as a whole whether someone is celebrating a birthday or an anniversary. Some will be too shy to acknowledge and others say they are celebrating when in fact the actual date may have been months earlier. This mistake can be costly if your company provides gifts for these occasions.)

- Have people draw names when they come in and let them know that during the cruise they must get to know the person whose name they drew. Then, at the farewell party, they are to give that person a small souvenir. They can purchase something on board or in port (set a value of about $2.00).

- If it is your style, have a sing-along. Provide the words of old favorites to the entire group.

Book and Magazine Swap

Many people bring paperbacks to read while cruising and then leave the books behind to make room in their luggage for souvenirs. Take advantage of this practice by holding a book swap, which I suggested bringing up at your initial briefing. Because many ships have limited libraries, your clients will appreciate the opportunity to have new reading materials.

Lending Library

Bring along some of your own favorite books about the areas you'll be visiting. These could include books about local customs, picture books on flowers or birds, books about or written by famous people from the area, poetry by well-known local poets or travel information books. For example: when touring Alaska, take along a book of poems by the bard of the Yukon, Robert M. Service, or a book by the author-adventurer Jack London. When in Hawaii take Michener's book on Hawaii. Let clients know they can check them out of your personal library.

Souvenir Swaps

Many people on vacation go crazy buying souvenirs; when they get home — and more often when they are packing at the end of the cruise — they wonder why they ever bought them. Here are two activities you can offer to help clients get rid of their unwanted souvenirs. Obviously, these work best late in the cruise, either at the final briefing or farewell party. Alternatively, you can set up a special time and place with the cruise director for these activities.

White Elephant Sale: Hold a white elephant sale (be sure it's not one of the ship's activities.) Run it like an auction. That is, have passengers put prices on the items they want to sell. Then you, the auctioneer, try to get that amount for each item. All the money goes to the passenger who contributed the item. *Never keep money for yourself.* A variation is simply to come and swap treasures. At least they get to think twice about what souvenirs they really want to take home.

Silent Auction: For a silent auction, ask clients to bring their sale items to you. Record who brought what. Place all items on a table with a pad and pencil next to each. Instruct people to write down their names and what they are willing to pay for the item. Have a time limit; the last name on the list buys the item. Check your list to be sure the money goes to the original owner.

Quizzes

As described in chapter 4, quizzes are entertaining and a good way to stay in contact with your passengers. They can be done by individuals, couples or teams. Use the quizzes described in chapter 4 or dream up some of your own. Prizes and rewards add to the enjoyment.

Games

- Arrange group tournaments such as shuffleboard, ping pong, bridge and backgammon. Or better yet, get a group together to participate in the ship's tournaments.

- Organize a scavenger hunt. Make a list of items for clients to find or information they will need to elicit from the crew — for example, a bartender's birthday or the captain's home country or city. This gets the passengers involved with the crew, which also enhances the cruise for the staff.

- Make a scramble game out of ships' names. Pass out a paper with the name of the ship (e.g., Star Princess) or the cruise, (e.g., China Dynasty Cruise) and ask clients to see how many words they can make out of the letters.

Prizes

Here are some suggestions for simple prizes to award the winners:

- Use the wine or champagne that some ships send to the cruise hosts and/or repeat travelers.
- If you have established a good relationship with the ship's photographers, ask them to donate a stock photo of the ship.
- Shop for inexpensive souvenirs during your port visits and use those as gifts.
- If you are really stuck, ask the ship's staff to provide you with small gifts. (Because these gifts will be the same as those handed out at all the ship's functions, make this a last-ditch choice. And, remember, it is not the ship's responsibility to provide your group with free gifts.)

Contributing Your Talents

If you have a particular talent or special interest and the ship is not holding a similar function, arrange that activity for your group. For example:

- Scarf tying
- Language lessons of the country to which you are traveling
- Dance lessons of the country to which you are traveling (Ask the crew to help you out on this one. They'll love it.)
- An informal talk on interesting customs or foods of the region or country.

The following involve the expertise of others but it is up to you to organize and/or manage them.

Group Photograph

Have the ship's photographer take a group photo. This brings the group together and obviously pleases the photographer. If you have a large group and there is a possibility of selling many copies, you may negotiate a client discount with the photographer. (*Never* request a commission for yourself.)

After the photo is taken, work with the photographer to promote sales. For example, arrange to get one copy of the photograph and carry it with you as you go about your daily routines. Some companies provide a group photo, but if they don't, when you see your clients, show them the photo. Have some order forms with you. This gives you another opportunity to do something extra for your group. It is also another chance to strike up a conversation with your passengers.

Private Tours

When you arrange any tour, deliver invitations to your clients the day before and indicate the time, date and place to meet. If your clients take a *private* tour, tell them not to announce it to the other passengers as this option may not be available to everyone on board.

Galley Tour: Sometimes the ship will have a scheduled galley tour for all passengers. If they don't, and, if you have a group of manageable size, you may be able to arrange a tour for them. Talk to the maitre d', the cruise director or, in some cases, even the shore excursion manager.

Bridge Visit: Most ships do have a bridge visit, but you still may be able to arrange a private visit for your group. If the ship does not have a standard bridge visit, it's worth trying to negotiate one. Check with the cruise director's office.

Cabin Tour: Some ships, depending on the occupancy rate, will have a tour of unoccupied cabins so clients can see different accommodations, such as mini-suites and suites. The cruise line does this in the hope that passengers will book an upgraded cabin on their next cruise. The cruise director, cruise consultant or passenger service representative may be willing to arrange a private showing for your group.

Engine Room Tour: Very few ships have an engine room tour and none offer it to all passengers. These tours are usually limited to 20 to 25 people who specifically ask to see the engine room. Talk to the shore excursions manager, cruise director or someone in the purser's office to see whether a private tour is possible for your group. You should be aware — and explain to your passengers — that this tour does not go to the actual working engine room, only to the control room. Be sure to check out access conditions to the control room. Many can be reached only by a steep ladder or stairs and are not appropriate for people who have difficulty balancing or climbing.

Activities the Ship Conducts

All cruise ships have countless activities for passengers. An important aspect of your job is to get your group to participate in as many events as possible. One way is to organize standing teams for pool games, shuffleboard and ping pong. (And remember: if you expect your people to participate, you must also participate.)

On one of my cruises the ship had a lip-sync party and a group of cruise hosts got together to lip-sync "For All the Girls I've Loved Before" sung by Willie Nelson and Julio Iglesias. When "Willie" and "Julio" came to the chorus of the song, ten pregnant women walked out on stage, one by one! It brought the house down. I've since used it with my cruise clients and they loved participating. You can also get your passengers involved as back-up or lead singers in a group.

Here are some other typical ship activities:

Horse Racing

Many ships hold a "Kentucky Derby" where wooden horses are auctioned, decorated by their new owners and placed in races. Make sure you talk to the social staff or cruise director to find out how your ship conducts these races. On some ships the staff advances the horses by rolling the dice; on others, participants advance the horses by pulling them in with fishing reels. You need to know the procedure so you can explain it to your people and get them excited about participating. Those who join in this activity always have a lot of fun.

First, get a group together to buy a horse. Let them establish beforehand the amount they are each willing to invest. (Horses can sell for $50 to $500). Once you've established the total the group wants to spend, have them bid on a horse at the auction. If they succeed in buying a horse, they must then get together to name it and decorate it. They will all share in the Derby festivities and possible cash rewards. Even if your group is outbid, they will still have had the fun of trying.

Masquerade Party

The ship's masquerade parties are always popular. Encourage your group to take part. If they have not brought along costumes, there are easy ways to create them on board. The ship provides the makings for costumes; they usually hand them out two or three days before the party. You can become very creative with what they give you and the things you and your passengers have brought from home.

Here are some costume suggestions.

Souvenir Man or Woman

On their outfit (skirt, slacks) a man or a woman pins, tapes or pastes on: postcards, small soaps from the ship, pictures, ship's newspaper, a menu from the dining room, stationery, souvenirs purchased from the countries visited. The more items that can be used the better.

The Perfect Wife

A woman dresses in pj's, nightgown, or sweatsuit, wears rollers in her hair, stuffs herself to look pregnant and goes barefoot. She carries a silver tray with a bottle and glass and holds a newspaper under her arm. Tape over her mouth creates the final effect. Don't forget a sign on her back saying "The Perfect Wife."

Tour Guide

A man or woman wears a hat with balloons, and holds up an umbrella, looking like he/she is in charge.

American Tourist

A man or woman with a life jacket swung over his/her back, camera around neck, money hanging out of pocket, carrying things purchased from countries visited and a long list of things to see, do or buy.

(These can be done individually or by a couple teaming up.)

Hershey's® Chocolate Bars

This one requires a man and a woman. Get two large black plastic garbage bags from the ship (or bring two with you). The woman puts her bag on with the light-colored side out and wears a sign saying "Hershey's Plain." The man wears the bag with the darker side out and a sign saying "Hershey's with Nuts."

Man Dressed as a Woman

This is pretty easy to do and needs no explanation. The crowd always loves it. Be creative!

Semi-Formal (Dressy on top and nothing on the bottom)

A man would wear a tuxedo top or sports coat, shirt, tie, socks, shoes and shorts, but no pants. A woman would dress in a dressy top (covering the hips), heels, but no skirt or slacks.

The Columbia Glacier in Alaska

A group of people wrap themselves together in bed sheets (all as one) carrying a sign that says Columbia Glacier (or whatever glacier you may have visited.)

Shipwrecked

You can usually get everything you need from the ship's staff: pirate hat, eye patch, beard, torn clothes. (Go barefoot and carry an empty booze bottle.)

Ship Theme

Create costumes that carry out a theme. It can relate to the ship, crew or destination ports. If the ship has a Greek crew, you might wear a toga. If you are in Hawaii, be a hula girl.

Talent Shows

Encourage anyone with talent to participate. It is also fun to do a group act. Here are some suggestions for groups:

- In Alaska you could stage your version of a melodrama (e.g., *The Cremation of Sam McGee,* by Robert Service). Someone can read the poem while others act it out. Or each person can read and act out his/her own character.

- Try an audience participation skit such as "Cowboys Courageous" (*Example 8.1*). Keep it light and funny and have a good time with it. Remember to tell your passengers that the worse they are the more the audience will love them.

- Sing a song as a group and get the audience to participate.

- Involve your group in making up a skit — about the trip, the area or the cruise.

- Teach your group.a line dance they can do to a popular song.

Cowboys Courageous

PURPOSE: Crowd breaker
MATERIALS: One copy of story
DIRECTIONS: Divide the audience into seven groups. Assign
the following parts to each group:
1. The Cowboys (shout Whooppee!)
2. The Indians (a-whoo-whoo-whoo) Indian war cry
3. The Women (Help me, Help me)
4. The Horses (Clippety-clop) with hands and feet
5. The Stagecoach (Giddy-up)
6. The Rifles (Bang! Bang!)
7. The Bows and Arrows (Zip, Zip) Do motions with hands

Each part requires no acting, only sound effects. The group assigned to each part simply makes the appropriate sound effect each time its part comes up in the story, which is read by the cruise host or a passenger in your group. The groups should try to outdo each other. The group that makes the most noise is the winner.

THE STORY:

It was in the days of **STAGECOACHES** and **COWBOYS** and **INDIANS**. Sagebrush Sam, Slim Chance, and Whip Lash were three courageous **COWBOYS**. When the **STAGE-COACH** left for Horseshoe Bend they were aboard, as were also two **WOMEN**: Ruby Red and a doll-faced brunette. The **STAGECOACH** was pulled by four handsome **HORSES**, and it left Roundtree Corners right on time.

The most treacherous part of the journey was the pass known as Gruesome Gulch. As the **STAGECOACH** neared this spot, one could tell that the **WOMEN** were a bit nervous while the **COWBOYS** were alert, fingering their **RIFFLES** as if to be ready for any emergency. Even the **HORSES** seemed to sense the danger.

Sure enough, just as the **STAGECOACH** entered the gulch, there sounded the blood curdling war cry of the **INDIANS**. Mounted on **HORSES**, they came galloping wildly toward the **STAGECOACH** shooting their **BOWS AND ARROWS**. The **COWBOYS** took careful aim with their **RIFLES** and fired repeatedly at the **INDIANS**. The **WOMEN** screamed. The **HORSES** pranced nervously. The **INDIANS** shot their **BOWS AND ARROWS**. The **COWBOYS** aimed the **RIFLES** again, shooting with deadly accuracy. The leading brave fell and the **INDIANS** turned their **HORSES** and raced off, leaving their **BOWS AND ARROWS** behind. The **WOMEN** fainted. The **COWBOYS** fired one more volley from their **RIFLES**. The driver urged on the **HORSES** and the **STAGECOACH** sped on toward Horseshoe Bend. The **WOMEN** were revived and showered the **COWBOYS** with praise for their heroic acts.

Example 8.1 Audience Participation - Cowboys Courageous

Karaoke Singing Machine

Many ships have installed a Karaoke singing machine in one of the small lounges or in the disco. These are machines that play music and display the words on a small TV-like screen. The machines come with music books that allow you to choose from thousands of songs. You can get your passengers to pick a song to perform as a group or encourage them to perform individually. Even if they don't participate, they will enjoy watching the others.

For all these ship activities, times and places will be listed in the ship's daily newspaper.

Chapter 9

Preparing for Special Occasions

Cruising has a party atmosphere, so you can use any excuse to decorate your clients' cabin doors and dining room tables. Here is where you can have a lot of fun and be very creative. Staff members will love it because decorations also brighten their day. The other passengers notice the special treatment your clients get and might wish they were with your group.

Door Decorations

The best time to decorate cabin doors for a holiday is the night before, once you are sure your clients have retired for the evening. When they open the door in the morning they will be pleasantly surprised. Using the basic supplies you brought along — balloons, streamers, banners, confetti and ribbon (see Party Supplies under "Supplies to Bring" in the appendix) — here are suggestions for creating special-occasion decorations.

Regardless of the occasion, you can always decorate cabin doors with a banner, appropriately colored streamers and balloons and a greeting card or some other personalized note to identify you and your company (*Example 9.1*). In addition to banners, streamers and balloons, here are some specific ideas for special-occasion or holiday decorations. Most you can make yourself using construction paper or you can purchase ahead of time at a party supply store:

Bon Voyage: Cardboard cut-out of a champagne bottle and wine glasses

Birthday / Anniversary: A cut-out of a wrapped package with a bow or a birthday cake with candles

Valentine's Day: Red cardboard hearts, shredded red ribbon, red or pink heart-shaped balloons, children's style Valentine cards, red paper doilies and Cupids

St. Patrick's Day: Green paper shamrocks or leprechauns

Easter: Cardboard bunnies, Easter eggs, Easter baskets

Mother's Day: "Happy Mother's Day" banner, Mother's Day card

Happy Birthday Beverly!
From Susie
Your Travel Time Hostess

Happy Birthday!

Example 9.1 Door Decoration

Father's Day: "Happy Father's Day" banner, Father's Day card

Fourth of July: American flag, stars and stripes

Halloween: Pumpkins, black cats, witches or ghosts

Thanksgiving: Turkeys, Pilgrims or cornucopias

Christmas / New Year's: Paper Santas, wreaths or Christmas trees. Candy canes, Christmas card, champagne bottles and glasses.

Table Decorations

As with door decorations, any occasion can be reason for decorating tables in the dining room. Incidentally, a good idea for many of the events listed below is to place a tent card in the center of the table. Whatever the occasion, just list on the card the names of your clients seated at that table. Always say "Compliments of" your company and your name (*Example 9.4*). Here are some table decorations I've used successfully; they might trigger some other thoughts for you.

Anniversary or Birthday: Attach a "Happy Anniversary" or "Happy Birthday" balloon to a stick, tie some curling ribbon around the stick (curl or shred the ribbon with a ribbon shredder) and place the stick in a vase at the client's table (*Example 9.2*). Sprinkle confetti on the table to give it a party atmosphere. (Be sure to ask the waiter for permission before you use confetti.) Again, make sure there is company identification on the table or on the balloon.

If one of your passengers is celebrating a special anniversary — a silver or golden — you may want to put some candles on the table. (Sometimes the ship can provide candles.) Assuming you thought of it ahead of time, get some flowers while in port, and place them in a vase on the table. Again, the cruise director or social staff can sometimes provide this. Try to find something funny or unusual on the ship to use as a vase.

Example 9.2 Table Balloon

You may want to blow up a balloon and place it with a banner and streamers outside the dining room door. Print the party person's name on the banner so they can see it upon entering.

Although not a table decoration, strictly speaking, arrange with the maitre d' for the ship to provide a complimentary cake when dessert is served. You may want to be there to add your greetings or to sing along when the cake is delivered. (Most ships will send a card signed by the captain.)

For major holidays, the ship does a bang-up job decorating tables in the dining room, but for other special occasions, table decorations also send the message to your clients that they matter to you. (Remember to use tent cards, especially if you have ship's passengers seated with your clients.)

Mother's Day / Father's Day: Although good for many occasions, I have used little "pinch toys" (*Example 9.3*) as remembrances for Mother's and Father's Day. In Australia they have koala bears; in China, panda bears. You can have the animals "hold" a small balloon or a greeting card. Place one at every woman's table setting for Mother's Day and every man's place for Father's Day. Or place a fresh flower, with ribbon tied around it, at each person's table setting — especially if you are in an area (like Bangkok or Hawaii) where flowers are both exotic and inexpensive. Stand a tent card (*Example 9.4*) with Happy Mother's Day or Father's Day in the center of the tables where your clients are seated. List clients' names and include "Compliments of" (your name and company).

Example 9.3
Panda Decoration

Happy Father's Day
John Smith
Bill Gray
Dave Anderson
Compliments of (Cruise Host Name)
Travel Time Tours

Example 9.4 Tent Card

Valentine's Day: Sprinkle pink and white heart-shaped confetti on the table. During your table rounds, place a chocolate heart on a small, red, heart-shaped paper doily at each table setting. Attach a heart-shaped balloon to a stick with lots of red and white curled or shredded ribbon. Place it in the vase on the table.

Easter: Put Easter "grass" and plastic eggs filled with jelly beans, or chocolate eggs (one for each client) at the center of the table. Or, put individual baskets with Easter grass and candy at each client's table setting. Place "Happy Easter" streamers on the table.

Some foreign countries have special gifts for Easter. In Brazil, for example, you can buy chocolate Easter eggs wrapped in pretty cellophane. These are the kinds of items you can purchase when you're in port — if your budget allows. You can put them on the dinner table for decoration or contact the cabin stewards to place them in your clients' cabins for you.

Halloween: Fill small Halloween bags with candy and place at each client's table setting. Put small gifts at each place setting — funny joke items like glasses with big eyes or a pop-on animal nose. (See appendix for suppliers.)

Christmas / New Year's: As mentioned, the ship does a great job with major holiday decorations in the dining room. You may want to just decorate cabin doors and leave the dining room tables to them. You could pass out candy canes to your clients during table rounds, if you would like to do something extra. All ships have huge celebrations for these holidays.

Gifts for Clients
For Special Occasions

Some companies give you a budget for birthday and anniversary gifts, usually $5 to $25 per person or event. Here are several gift ideas to help celebrate these occasions:

- A bottle of wine. Be sure to find out whether the person drinks by asking the dining room wine steward what kind of wine has been ordered so far at their table. If no wine has been ordered, you can buy a nonalcoholic wine. Deliver it to the dining room table or to the client's cabin. (I used to always send wine to the table directly, but some people don't want to share with their table mates. If you send wine to their cabin, they can choose to celebrate alone or take their wine to the table for dinner.)

- A gift certificate for one or more photos taken by the ship's photographer. (The quantity depends on how much you can spend.)
- A photo of your client with the captain or a photo of your client that you think is particularly good — framed or unframed.
- A ship's photo album.
- A tote bag from the ship or a souvenir tote bag from a port.
- Any souvenir — T-shirt, scarf, towel, picture book of the area or local specialty (candy or perfume) — from one of the ports visited.

For the End of the Trip

Again, if your budget allows, plan to pick up small gifts from the ports visited during the cruise. Different countries and regions are known for certain specialty items. Many are under $1. Hold on to these presents until the end of the tour and use them as farewell gifts. Some suggestions in that price range are:

Australia: pinch toy (koala)

Greece: small hand-painted plate

China: pinch toy (panda)

Holland: ceramic "wooden shoe" pins

Nova Scotia: paper flower (wild aster)

Bear in mind that people must pack these gifts, so keep them small, unbreakable and packable. You can hand them out at the final briefing or farewell party, or you can use them to decorate clients' tables on the final night of the cruise. If you place them on the tables be sure to also include a thank-you note or tent card, as well.

Chapter 10

Working with On-Board Staff

Next to satisfying the needs of your clients, one of your most important jobs is to create a good working relationship with the on-board staff. Staff members are there to provide service to you and your clients. Don't abuse their good graces. Be willing to work on their terms. Be tactful, polite, understanding and appreciative at all times. Staff members have their own jobs to do. Although they are perfectly willing to work with cruise hosts, they do not take well to cruise hosts who are demanding, pushy or otherwise unprofessional. They appreciate cruise hosts who are organized, dress appropriately and care about the passengers.

Remember also that the ship is the staff's home and office. Don't make yourself too much at home in their space. Their privacy should be respected at all times. How you act and work with staff members will also influence how they treat the next cruise host who comes on board.

Do's and Don'ts

Most of these bits of advice have already been mentioned in previous sections, but they bear repeating.

The Do's

- Introduce yourself to all staff members as soon as possible and be sure to remember their names. Ask how you can best accomplish your goals in a way that also works for them.

- If you can't find staff members you need to meet, write personal notes introducing yourself and saying that you are looking forward to meeting and working with them. Leave the notes in their offices.

- When you invite staff members to your cocktail parties, deliver personal invitations the day before the event. Sometimes that gesture, alone, is the reason they attend. Address the envelope with their names and not just their titles.

- The staff will appreciate it greatly if your clients participate in the ship's on-board activities. Participation makes the cruise more fun for the staff, for your clients and for all cruise passengers. Encourage your passengers to join in.

- Attend the entertainment programs and ship's activities yourself whenever possible. If you show an interest, the performers and staff will be much friendlier toward you. Being at these functions also signals to your clients that ship events are worth participating in or attending.

- Anytime you need photocopies, offer to make them yourself. If you encounter problems with using the copier, wait to locate a copier in port. The staff may be too busy to assist you. Always be aware that you are in their domain.

- Staff members do not have unlimited expense accounts on the ship. If they buy you a drink, do be sure to reciprocate.

- Be organized, offer sincere compliments to the staff and SMILE! It's a good idea when there's a problem to say: "What can *we* do about it?"

The Don'ts

- Although you are a cruise host, staff members must treat you like a passenger. That means not saying anything to you directly if you upset them or get in their way. Be aware of your actions and make sure they are in harmony with the ship. If you have a problem, locate the right person to assist you — always with a big smile and a lot of patience.

- Don't look for discounts and freebies for yourself (from the staff, ships photographer, boutique, etc.) That is not professional.

- Never interrupt staff members when they are talking with someone else. Wait until they acknowledge you.

- Know where you can and can't go on the ship. For example, if you want to send a TELEX and you are asked to leave it at the front desk, leave it at the front desk; don't go directly to the radio room.

- Don't use the ship's Scotch tape, correction fluid, paper or party supplies. The ship's limited supplies are not easily replaced. (See the office and party supply lists in the appendix so you'll know what to bring with you.)

- Don't be upset if you are not invited to parties for travel agents, repeat passengers and so on. It is probably an oversight and not worth making a fuss over. Don't risk alienating the staff.

- When you attend the captain's cocktail party conduct yourself as a guest, not a cruise host. Because you are a cruise host and may have clients at both cocktail parties (first and second seating), the captain will not mind if you attend both the first and second seating parties. Don't, however, stand outside to greet your clients. It is okay to sit and talk with them, but don't act as social hostess. This is the captain's party!

- Don't be upset if the captain or staff members do not attend your welcome or farewell cocktail party. They may be on duty at the time. Keep in mind, when the ship pulls in or out of port, the captain must be on the bridge.

- On embarkation day, don't ask the ship's staff (located on the dock) to change cabin assignments. They can't do it. Cabin assignments can't be changed until the ship has sailed and cabin status is known. At that time the hotel manager will be your contact.

- Never bad-mouth the staff. They are a very close-knit family and if you alienate one, you alienate all. They can be critical of one another but don't you join in. Even when staff treats you like one of the family, you do not have the same privileges. Also, don't expect to be included in any of their free-time activities. Staff members need this private time.

- Be careful in your relations with crew members. The ship is a very small community. If you date one crew member, everyone knows. You may think you are being discreet but the entire ship will hear of it in a day!

Some Key Staff Members
Maitre d'

As discussed in some detail in chapter 5, establishing and maintaining a good working relationship with the maitre d' is critical to your success as a cruise host. So get to know him early and learn to work with him. A good working relationship will ensure your clients' dining satisfaction.

It is very important to make a good impression on the maitre d'. You will be asking him favors throughout the cruise, such as:

- Making table changes (sometimes several times)
- Concocting special meals
- Celebrating birthdays and anniversaries
- Conducting galley tours

On your first meeting with the maitre d' (embarkation day) you will be obtaining your clients' table numbers and seating requests. Maitre d's have their own ways of working. You should be aware that:

- The maitre d' may have your group on a separate list. Ask whether you can see the list to copy the table numbers assigned to your passengers (then transfer those table numbers to your dining room seating request chart (*Example 3.2*).
- The maitre d' may ask you to call out your group's cabin numbers or last names. He will then give you the corresponding table numbers.
- The maitre d' may ask you to meet with him on the first morning after embarkation when he will give you your table numbers. If this is the case you will not be able to contact your clients on the first night of the cruise. This sometimes makes clients feel neglected. Let your people know at the initial briefing (see chapter 6) that it was not possible to contact them on the first evening without their dining room table numbers.
- The maitre d' may be located on the dock on embarkation day. If so, you can obtain table numbers before boarding the ship. This is the exception, however.
- The maitre d' will have placed a dining room seating table reservation card in the passengers' cabins (*Example 10.1* and *10.2*). This will inform them of their table number and whether they have first or second seating. As cruise host, you may not have a table assignment prior to boarding. When you meet with the maitre d' let him know which seating you want and whether or not you want to sit with your passengers or with other cruise hosts. (Again, it is not suggested that you sit with your clients.) *Example 10.1* simply tells the seating and table number and lists the time of meals. *Example 10.2* shows an actual diagram of the dining room so that clients can find their tables prior to coming to dinner.

2nd Seating

You Are Seated at Table No. _____

Breakfast at 8:00 a.m.

Lunch at 1:15 p.m.

Dinner at 8:15 p.m.

Breakfast Buffet 8:00 A.M. - 9:30 a.m.

Your promptness will help to facilitate more efficient service.

Thank you

Example 10.1 Dining Room Table Reservation Card

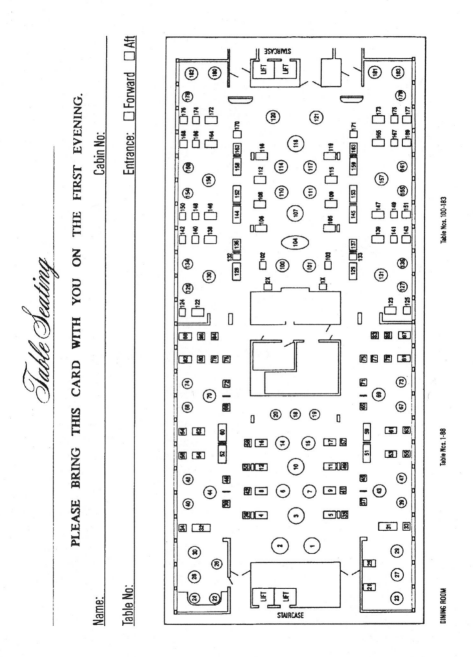

Example 10.2 Dining Room Table Reservation Card with Layout

If you are tipping the maitre d' for your group, tip him at the beginning, toward the middle or at the end of the cruise. It is not advisable to give him half at the beginning and hold out the other half until the end of the cruise. To do so implies that he has to prove himself. Assume that he will give you excellent service.

On some ships the captain takes his meals in the dining room throughout the cruise. He may dine only with his staff or he may invite passengers to dine with him. This honor is usually reserved for special people or special occasions. If you have clients who are celebrating an important birthday or anniversary, ask the maitre d' if they may join the captain for dinner. Keep in mind, however, that on many ships, passengers are never asked to join the captain's table.

Captain

Although a key person on the ship, the captain is actually not someone that you as a cruise host have a great deal to do with in working with your group.

Also, as far as your relationship with the captain is concerned keep in mind when planning your parties that the captain has first choice. He will usually have his welcome cocktail party the second or third night out, depending on which day the ship will be in port and the time the ship sails. If the ship has a farewell cocktail party, it is usually held two or three nights before the end of the cruise. It is very unusual for the captain to have a formal farewell party on the last night of a cruise.

Cruise Director

The cruise director will be setting the times and places for many of your group's functions. If you familiarized yourself with the ship, you will know all the public spaces and their capacities and will have decided in advance which room(s) you want for your functions, based on the size of your group. Have a second choice ready in case the space you want is unavailable.

If you have read the ship's newspaper, you will have an idea of available times for your scheduled events. Check that these times don't conflict with ship functions. Never book a briefing, party or other gathering during important ship's functions such as port talks, shore excursion briefings, embarkation and disembarkation talks and captain's cocktail parties. And, *never, never* book anything during bingo, especially snowball jackpot bingo!

Always keep in mind that the cruise director is very busy and usually needs to be in three places at the same time. Be well organized when meeting with a cruise director.

Bar Manager

Any time you're holding an event where drinks are to be served, you may have to consult directly with the bar manager. Again, be organized and have all your requests ready, and be flexible. Request a private room for your functions. If you have a large group, avoid booking a party in the showroom where three or four groups may be having a party at the same time. Using a public room with multigroup parties works only with small groups, and even then it is not the ideal situation.

Hotel Manager and Head Housekeeper

The hotel manager is the person to see if your clients want to change or upgrade their cabins. Just because clients are angry and threatening to leave the cruise, do not try to appease them by upgrading their cabin as compensation. The hotel manager knows from experience that a cabin upgrade is not a miracle cure for an angry client.

He also handles any cabin maintenance problems (plumbing, telephone, air conditioning, etc). The hotel manager will most likely turn these problems over to the head housekeeper or cabin stewards; so if you have struck up friendly relationships with these staff members you can go to them directly. (The head housekeeper works miracles with problems like damaged luggage, also.)

Passenger Service Representatives

Although not all ships have passenger service representatives (PSRs), those that do assign them a major role on the cruise. They are responsible for solving all passenger problems — from lost and damaged luggage to airline seating and ticketing problems. Besides handling problems, PSRs are responsible for collecting airline tickets and for reconfirming airline flights. Sometimes they seat the plane on the cruise line's charter flights, and they must organize and distribute baggage tags and possibly boarding passes for the return flight. If you have a passenger who must leave the cruise, the PSR will help you arrange for flights and transfers. The PSR may also be the person who does the final disembarkation talk.

The PSR's job is a very stressful one. They take a great deal of abuse from upset passengers. Treat them well; they will play a very important role on your cruise.

Shore Excursion Manager and Staff

The shore excursion staff have a very difficult and demanding job. They work long hours selling and organizing shore excursions. They call ahead to the local ground operator with final passenger counts, pull tickets and sometimes personally deliver tickets to the passengers' cabins. It is sometimes difficult to work with clients who are disappointed if a particular shore excursion they wanted is sold out. "After all, that was the only reason we came on this cruise."

The shore excursion manager also decides whether a group buy is possible, and they have the final say on whether you as cruise host will have a complimentary tour. Don't rush up to the shore excursion office to ask for complimentary tours. Get to know the staff first, and be understanding if they can't accommodate you.

All ships have their own way of dealing with complimentary shore excursions for cruise hosts:

- Complimentary shore excursions may be included as part of the contract your company has with the cruise line.
- The shore excursion staff may ask you what tours you want and then assign you and other staff members to represent the cruise line as group escorts. Sometimes they will ask you to carry a first aid kit or to fill out a report about the shore excursion.
- They may ask you to wait to see whether any seats are left on the coaches. If not, be gracious about it.
- On some ships you may have to pay passenger rates for all your shore excursions.

On the Ship

As a cruise host, these are some suggestions for working with the shore excursion staff:

1. As soon as possible after boarding, ask the shore excursion manager whether a group buy is possible. If so, offer your services (pulling tickets, delivering them to the cabins, etc.) Ask them how they want you to prepare the shore excursion orders and then follow their procedure. Shore excursions are usually charged directly to the cabins so no money transactions are required. In fact, if the shore excursions require payment in cash, do not attempt a group buy. You do not want to be responsible for cash transactions with your clients.

2. When you go to the shore excursion office for the group buy, don't wear your name badge. This is not a good time for other passengers to know who you are. They will resent the fact that you don't have to wait in line to get tickets. Discretion is critical.

3. If you are given a complimentary shore excursion, write a short report about the tour for the shore excursion staff. Highlight the good points as well as the problem areas. Be constructive. Constructive criticism is fine. If your free shore excursion was arranged by the shore excursion manager, be sure to write a thank-you note.

On the Dock

1. Try to be one of the first people off the ship. Sum up the situation on the dock: where the coaches are, how to get a taxi, where the phones are, how to walk to town. Then, as your clients come off the ship you will be there to direct them correctly and to wish them a good day. Again, let the shore excursion staff know you are willing to help if they need you.

2. If you plan to be on the dock to see your clients off, don't stand at the end of the gangway. You could interfere with the dispatch of passengers and coaches. It is the shore excursion staff's job to get those coaches dispatched and on their way on time. The ship is on a strict time schedule in port and the tours must return on time. Never do anything to interfere with the flow of traffic. Similarly, if photographers are taking photos on the pier, do not get in the way.

3. Don't act as if you are dispatching the coaches. It is okay to greet your clients, direct them to the proper coaches and even arrange a taxi for them. Remember, however, that the other passengers will think you are part of the cruise staff and will also start asking you questions. Sometimes the shore excursion people are thankful for your help, but take care not to take over the situation.

4. If the staff doesn't want you on the dock, pick a lounge or someplace on the ship near the disembarkation point. Then let your clients know that if they need to see you, this is where you will be prior to all shore excursions.

Courtesies to Ship's Staff

You can (and should) find ways to express your appreciation to the ship's staff. For example, if they have gone out of their way for you or arranged special events:

- Deliver a note to their office with some chocolates (kisses) or other thoughtful, inexpensive gift.

- Invite them to all your cocktail parties and introduce them to your group. Tell your passengers what their jobs are on board and mention any special arrangements the staff has made to enhance their cruise.

- Write personal notes at the end of the cruise letting them know how much you enjoyed working with them.

On a Scandinavian cruise, another cruise host and I wanted to do something special for the social staff, who had been extremely helpful to us during the cruise. While sightseeing in Copenhagen, we remembered having passed a wonderful pastry shop displaying a vast assortment of delicious desserts. We purchased a huge box of pastries and, once back on board, attached to it a large rabbit balloon we had bought at Tivoli Gardens on a previous night. We then placed the whole package in the cruise staff's office, with a thank-you card. You might think it strange to give the staff food — after all, they get everything they want on the ship. But, they were thrilled and, believe me, they were happy to have a treat that was so much more delectable than the ship's standard fare.

Chapter 11

Handling Problems

Handling problems is a major responsibility for all ship's staff, and, as a professional cruise host, you will have your share. Many can be handled by using good common-sense judgment; others rely on your knowing as much as you can about how cruise lines work in general and your ship in particular. This chapter will discuss your clients' concerns as well as problems you may encounter.

Your Clients' Problems
Flight Bookings

Knowing how the cruise line works will help you explain problems to your clients. You won't always be able to "fix it" but you can at least provide them with information that might soothe ruffled feathers. Here are some common sources of complaints, a brief explanation of how the cruise line books its ships, and suggestions for handling angry clients.

Airline Schedules: The cruise line may have to book flights that are not the most direct or convenient for your clients. Many times your clients think that it is your company's fault and are angry when they arrive on the ship. Remember that airlines make air schedules, not the cruise line. Cruise lines, however, do try to get the best, most economical seats on the flights. These are called "contract fares." The airline will not allow any deviations or changes on contract fares because they pre-book blocks of seats based on the number of people they expect or actually have flying from each area. When an airline doesn't offer a contract fare on a direct flight, the cruise line may use many connecting flights to get clients to the embarkation point. In this case, again, they will try to obtain the best possible fare.

Cruise lines sometimes use block seating for passengers leaving from hub cities. For example, they may block 100 seats from Dallas/Fort Worth to Acapulco. To use the seats they blocked, they must put clients on flights from New York, Boston, Chicago and San Francisco to connect with the Dallas flight.

Direct flights are available only from gateway cities. Often clients will not get direct flights from their homes to the embarkation point because they do not live in the gateway city for the airline providing the flight.

Pre- and Post-Tour Flights: Cruise lines use pre-and post-tour packages for several reasons, the most important being to avoid having 1,000 passengers flying to the same destination on the same day.

A pre-or post-tour is also referred to as a rest-over stop because it provides passengers flying from any long distance a chance to rest for a night. This way they can board the ship the next day feeling more refreshed for their vacation. The cruise line generally does not make money on these tours; they offer them only as an enhancement to the cruise vacation.

Some cruise lines will allow passengers to fly to or from the embarkation or disembarkation port one or two days in advance or at the end of the cruise. They usually charge a small amount for this deviation. They cannot make major changes to accommodate individual clients because to do so would drastically change the fare structure they contracted for. Cruise lines don't want to act as travel agencies.

Return Flights: If clients did not have good flights *to* the ship, they often spend the entire cruise worrying about their return flights. As cruise host, you can explain the ship's procedures and reduce their anxieties. First find out from the passenger service representative or someone from the cruise director's office whether the ship's staff will be seating the return flight. The staff usually seats the plane if the cruise line has chartered the return flight; otherwise, the airline chooses the seats. In that case it is out of everyone's control. If the ship's staff seats the plane, you can request a special seat for a client and usually get it. The staff tries its best, and with charter flights the staff has the final say. This is one of the places where a good working relationship with the staff means a lot to your effectiveness with your group.

Despite who does the seating, the ship's staff usually does not return tickets, release seat assignments or hand out boarding passes (if they are available) until the very end of the cruise. The reasons for this are (1) they don't want passengers to lose them, and (2) because there is nothing they can do to change seating assignments at this point, they don't want last-minute complaints.

Cabin Problems

If clients are not satisfied with their cabins or do not think they got what they paid for, find out if they are truly unhappy or are just trying for a free upgrade. Say to them, "I know that you are unhappy with your cabin. I would like to do something for you. If I can find you a better cabin, would you be willing to pay the difference?" Usually, if they are truly dissatisfied, they will be willing to pay. You can convey this information to the hotel manager. Your chances for a cabin change for this type of client are far better than for a client who is just a complainer.

Dining Room Seating Requests

Sometimes passengers get second seating when they wanted first or first when they requested second. If first seating is overbooked, promote second seating. There are many reasons why second seating is better: Your clients won't be so rushed to get out of the dining room, they don't have to rush back to the ship early from a shore excursions and they won't be rushed out of the showroom to make room for the second show. In fact, you might tell them that the only serious drawback to second seating is that they may be too full for the midnight buffet! If *second* seating is full, promote first seating: For example, tell them they'll be getting service while the waiters are fresh and they will have room for the midnight buffet!

Cruise Reservations

If clients booked one year in advance and later had problems with their bookings, first find out whether they made any recent changes. Such changes often alter their status and may disqualify any special rate they received on their original reservation.

If you come across a passenger who says your tour operator told them there was no space when, according to the client, the cruise line did have available cabins, you should explain that this can occur when the tour operator exceeds its allotment of cabins, or when the cruise line takes back unbooked space 60 to 90 days before the cruise and, as a result, ends up having space to sell.

Lost Airline Tickets

It is not uncommon for clients to lose their airline tickets, although nine times out of ten they will find them just before (or just after) the flight. When the tickets are issued by the cruise line, the ship's staff may be able to get the necessary information regarding the lost ticket or see that a new ticket is issued. As cruise host, you can also TELEX your office or the port agent and let them arrange with the airline for a prepaid ticket.

Sometimes clients will be going directly from the ship to the airport at the end of a cruise, and sometimes they will remain in a disembarkation city before returning home. Your options for handling these situations differ accordingly:

From Ship to Airport: At the end of a cruise some clients go directly from the ship to the airport and will have no time to replace a lost ticket. In that case, the airline will require the client to purchase a new full-fare one-way ticket, usually charged on a credit card. Some airlines will require passengers to fill out a Lost Ticket Refund Application *(Example 11.1)* and to list ticket numbers. Ticket numbers can be obtained from the local port agent's office and sometimes from the Passenger Services Representative on the ship, providing the cruise line is the issuing agent.

Without ticket numbers some airlines will not refund any portion of the ticket price. Some airlines will refund the full amount of the new ticket if it was purchased 55-70 days from the date of the original flight, providing the lost ticket has not been used. Assist clients by calling the airline and asking for the group desk or a supervisor to find out how they handle such situations. If there is no time for a phone call, accompany your passengers to the airport (if time allows) and help them make arrangements for a new ticket with the airlines. If that is not possible, inform your clients of the airline's procedures. This way they will know what to expect when they arrive at the ticket counter at the airport.

Remaining in the Final Disembarkation City: You have a better chance of taking care of a lost ticket problem if your group is staying in the final disembarkation city for a day or two before the flight home. You still fill out the Lost Ticket Application Form and you still need the lost ticket numbers. To get them, try the following:

- Call the airline. They can TELEX the issuing agent who will be able to provide the lost ticket numbers.

- Look in the white pages of the telephone book for the name and number of the cruise line's local port agency, or prior to disembarkation, you may be able to obtain the number from the cruise staff. The port agent can get you ticket numbers within a matter of minutes and may, if there is enough time, be able to get the ticket reissued before flight time. Be sure to ask.

- As a last resort, call your company's operations agent and ask them to trace the ticket numbers. Again, the port agent can give you ticketing information if the tickets were issued through the cruise line. Unless the cruise line can get the ticket reissued, or the airline is willing to reissue it (sometimes with a $50 service charge), the client will have to charge a new ticket on a credit card and wait for the refund. Be sure to find out whether the airline will reimburse the full amount of the new ticket purchased as long as the old ticket was not used. This policy varies from airline to airline.

Lost Ticket Refund Application

UNITED AIRLINES

Address correspondence to: United Airlines, Passenger Refunds-EXOAK, P.O. Box 66282, Chicago, Illinois 60666

VALIDATION STAMP

Claims will be processed in 55-70 days.
No claims will be processed until the ticket number is identified.

The undersigned applicant requests a refund of the value of the unused portion of the United Air Lines, Inc., ticket described below and, in requesting this refund, hereby *represents that the ticket is owned by the applicant and has not been used by him, and that it has been lost, stolen, or destroyed.*

✳ ✳ LOST TICKET INFORMATION (ONLY ONE PER APPLICATION) ✳

ISSUING AIRLINE	AIRLINE	FORM	SERIAL NUMBER

PASSENGER'S PHONE NO.

PORTION OF TICKET LOST WAS
From   To   CPN NO(S).

PASSENGER'S NAME (PRINT)

CITY WHERE PURCHASED

PAY REFUND TO

DATE OF PURCHASE   OR APPROXIMATELY BETWEEN   AND

NUMBER AND STREET

LOCATION OF SELLING OFFICE IN CITY WHERE PURCHASED (IF TRAVEL AGENT, SHOW NAME AND ADDRESS)

CITY, STATE, ZIP CODE

AMOUNT PAID FOR LOST TICKET
$

FORM OF PAYMENT OF LOST TICKET
☐ CASH   ☐ GR-NO.
☐ CHECK   ☐ OTHER
☐ CREDIT CARD ACCOUNT NO:

✳ ✳ ✳ ✳ ✳ REPLACEMENT TICKET INFORMATION ✳ ✳ ✳ ✳ ✳

AIRLINE	FORM	SERIAL NUMBER	DATE ISSUED

WAS ANY PORTION USED BEFORE LOSS?
☐ YES   ☐ NO

ISSUED AT | FROM | TO

USED
From   To

FLIGHT NUMBER | DATE | VALUE $

FLIGHT NUMBER	CLASS	DATE	DEPARTURE TIME

WAS REPLACEMENT TICKET PURCHASED? ☐ YES ☐ NO
ISSUED IN EXCHANGE FOR LTA? (REQUIRES SUPERVISOR'S APPROVAL) ☐ YES ☐ NO

LOST TICKET WAS LIFTED IN ERROR ON FLIGHT NO. | DATE

WAS THIRTY-FIVE DOLLAR ($35.00) SERVICE CHARGE COLLECTED? ☐ YES ☐ NO

1. The applicant understands and agrees that:

   A. A THIRTY-FIVE DOLLAR ($35.00) SERVICE CHARGE PER TICKET WILL BE ASSESSED FOR HANDLING THIS APPLICATION.

   B. This claim will be given consideration provided that the application has been made not later than one month after the expiration date of the lost ticket.

   C. THIS CLAIM WILL BE PROCESSED IN 55-70 DAYS AFTER RECEIPT OF THE COMPLETED APPLICATION IN THE EXECUTIVE OFFICES OF UNITED AIRLINES. REFUND WILL NOT BE MADE IF THE LOST TICKET HAS PREVIOUSLY BEEN HONORED FOR TRANSPORTATION OR REFUND TO ANY PERSON.

   D. United Air Lines, Inc., does not assume any liability for failure to identify the person used or presenting a ticket for refund as being the true owner of the ticket.

   E. Upon finding the lost ticket, the applicant will immediately send the ticket and a statement that a lost ticket application was filed to United Air Lines, Inc., Passenger Refunds, P.O. Box 66282, Chicago, Illinois 60666.

   F. This claim will be given consideration if the complete form and serial number of the lost ticket can be identified. If additional information is required to identify the lost ticket, United Airlines will communicate with you.

   G. Lost tickets purchased by Government Transportation Request are refundable only to the U.S. Government.

2. The applicant agrees to indemnify and hold United Air Lines, Inc., harmless against any and all loss, damage, claim or expense, including, without limitation, reasonable attorney's fees, which United Air Lines, Inc., may suffer or incur by reason for the making of such refund and/or the subsequent presentation of said ticket for transportation, refund or any other use whatsoever.

3. A refund issued as a result of this application may be subject to recall of commission if a replacement ticket was not purchased.

PLEASE ALLOW 55-70 DAYS FOR PROCESSING.   Please read the terms of this application before signing.

APPROVED BY LOCAL OFFICE SUPERVISOR | SIGNATURE OF PASSENGER (OR APPLICANT IF COMPANY IS CLAIMANT) | DATE

UA209 REV. 5/87 PRINTED IN U.S.A.   1. EXOAK – PASSENGER REFUNDS
2. PASSENGER

Example 11.1 Lost Ticket Refund Application

Payments

When a client books a cruise with your company, usually the cruise line will prepare the documents and send them to your tour operator. As mentioned earlier, it is your company's responsibility to send the documents to the client. This leaves much room for miscommunication, however. The cruise line often does not get back to the tour operator with reservation information until the last minute; the client then becomes worried and calls the cruise line directly to see when their tickets will arrive. This situation can create problems. For example, the cruise line usually receives one check from the tour operator for the entire group booking. An individual client is not aware that to get proper information they must talk to the *group department.* A reservations agent is not likely to have knowledge of payment and may not think to ask whether the client is with a group. The client, understandably, becomes upset if told there is no record of payment — which can happen with a group booking that delays posting payments to individual accounts. When this happens, clients lose confidence in your company.

Dealing with an Angry Client

Whatever problems you face, general rules for dealing with an angry client are:

- Let them vent! You don't have to agree with them, but you should acknowledge their feelings and keep your cool. Show concern. Remain objective. Make sure you understand the real problem. Ask what they would like you to do. Remember, most people don't sees themselves as part of the problem.

- After listening and acknowledging what they have to say, give them 24 hours (if possible) before approaching them again. This will give them a chance to cool off. (If you have a solution, of course, give it to them as soon as possible.)

- If the problem was created by the cruise line (flight or cabin assignments), tell the client you'll talk with the ship's staff. If the problem or complaint is legitimate, you may be able to get the ship to send your client a bottle of wine or some other compensation. (Several staff members can authorize sending wine: cruise director, assistant cruise director, passenger service representative, social hostess or hotel manager.) Some people create problems because they have learned it is a way to get free bottles of wine and because it has worked for them in the past. Whether or not the problem is justified, this token gift may ease the immediate anger — but it never solves the problem. Your personal concern will be a far better solution in the long run.

- Avoid saying to a client "It is company policy," "I'll try," "but," or "never." These expressions always have a negative impact.

Dealing with Clients Who Bad-Mouth the Cruise

If you have a problem client who is disrupting the entire ship by bad-mouthing the cruise or your company, (maybe as a result of a drinking problem) or is being abusive or disruptive to others, you need to control the problem as soon as possible. Try talking with the passenger to find out what the real or perceived problem is so you can maybe turn the person around and have them enjoy their cruise. If the person continues to be disruptive, contact the cruise director. Keep in mind that it is very hard to put a passenger off the ship. As far as your company is concerned, a passenger would have to agree, in writing, to leave the cruise. As far as the cruise line or ship is concerned, it has to be a threatening situation before they will put a passenger off the ship. When it must be done, it is the captain's decision, but he will not want to take the responsibility and this solution should *not* be regarded as an option. In other words, do everything you can to resolve the problem.

Your Own Problems
Not Having Your Own Cabin

Recently cruises have been selling out; often they don't have private cabins for professional cruise hosts. Unfortunately, cruise lines and tour operators don't yet fully understand the importance of cruise hosts having private cabins regardless of the loss of passenger revenue. Remember, tour operators generally receive one free berth for every 15 passengers booked; so, if they sell 30 passengers, they get two berths, which represents one full cabin. Many tour operators sell the free berth to make extra profit.

You should find out the policy of your tour operator and, if necessary, stress the value of your having a private cabin. For example, explain that (1) it will be very hard to do your work and keep your paperwork confidential, (2) your hours are not normal and you have many disruptions from phone calls and people knocking at the door, (3) your schedule is bound to antagonize your shipmate, and (4) you need quiet time and space to recharge your batteries.

One solution some tour operators employ is to pay a travel agent rate for your cabin (which can range from $200 to $1,000 depending on the cruise line and cabin category) and then sell the free berth for the full amount. The cruise line may have a policy disallowing this practice, however. Furthermore, if the ship is full or overbooked no cabins will be available at the travel agent rate.

Rooming with a Client or with Another Passenger

If your tour operator has not booked a single cabin for you and you end up rooming with a passenger or client, see the hotel manager as soon as possible and explain your situation. This is an impossible situation and must be avoided at all costs. If the ship is not overbooked, you will usually be accommodated.

If you simply must share, it is critical that you not inconvenience your shipmate. If you create a problem for that person, everyone on the ship will know. It will not speak well of you or of your company.

Rooming with Another Cruise Host

Although a better solution — at least you will be with someone who can understand your situation and what you are up against — problems can still occur. It will be just as hard to keep your documents and paperwork confidential. You will not have the privacy you need to re-energize, and, in addition, you may experience feelings of competition.

Chapter 12

Death of a Client

It may surprise you to know that it is a rare cruise when at least one passenger does not die. When the death involves your client, you must be there to assist.

Your responsibilities at this time are to provide emotional and practical support to the surviving spouse or traveling companion and to assist the ship's staff and/or port agents with the paperwork that must be taken care of — and quickly. (The captain's obligation is to keep the cruise on schedule. Disrupting the ship's schedule for any reason not only upsets passengers but is costly to the cruise line.) Remember that this situation will be emotionally trying not only to the surviving party or cruise-mate but to others in your group. Insofar as you can, reassure the rest of the group that you and the ship's personnel have everything under control.

The way things are handled differs depending on whether the death occurs on the ship or on the shore. In the first instance, your contacts are with the doctor and the purser; they keep the captain informed and contact the port agent in the next port. If the death occurs in port, you will assist ship's staff in dealing with the port agents of the country in which the death occured. They are the people who make the necessary arrangements for the body, conforming to whatever local laws and customs regulations apply. They also arrange for hotel and transportation for the survivor or companion and handle all of the local reports required. When a death occurs in port, during a shore excursion, for example, someone from the ship's staff should notify you. Most ships will not, for legal reasons, allow the body back on board.

What the Doctor Does

If you are the first one to learn of a client's death, immediately contact the ship's doctor. Only the ship's doctor can pronounce the person legally dead. If the ship is in international waters, the doctor is required to fill out the necessary reports and notify the captain or staff captain who, in turn, contacts the port agent at the nearest port.

The physician's staff is also responsible for preparing the body. Most ships have a morgue on board — freezer space designated for this purpose. For ships that don't, they use a freezer in the galley or even a tub of ice in one of the free (locked) cabins. Whatever needs to be done to preserve the body until the ship reaches port and until the survivor makes a decision on the disposition of the body is handled by the ship's doctor and staff.

Disposition of the Body

If the surviving party is a family member, that person must decide which option to use in disposing of the body:

- sending it home by plane

- burying the deceased in the country of death or the next port

- having the body cremated (in some countries cremation is mandatory)

- requesting a burial at sea

Burial at sea is a very tricky subject. Legally, it can be done. It will depend very much on the circumstances. If a passenger dies of a heart attack and there is no question of foul play, or if the survivor (who must be next of kin or husband or wife) insists they want the body buried at sea, then the decision is in the hands of the captain. Sometimes a spouse will argue that the next port is a country where it is mandatory to have the body cremated, and the survivor does not want that. As long as the ship is at least three miles away from any country, and the survivor has completed all the legally required paperwork to protect the cruise line, the captain could agree to a burial at sea. You should be aware, however, that this option is not a normal solution or even an easy one, and should not be encouraged. If there is any suspicion of foul play, local authorities may insist on holding the body for an autopsy. Similarly, in some countries a family member must make a report at the local police station as assurance that no foul play was involved.

If no family member is on board (a traveling companion cannot make these decisions) then you must locate the closest relative. Refer to the emergency information on your confidential client information sheets (*Example 2.4*). Or, call your tour operator's 24-hour emergency number. (More on that later.) Be aware that in many countries the ship is not permitted to leave the body in port until the decision about its disposition has been made.

What the Purser Needs

Whether the death occurs at sea or in port, the purser's office will need to have the passport of the deceased immediately in order to fill out the legal papers required by the cruise line and port agents.

Your Tasks

Below is a summary list of the practical steps you need to take for the survivor, the ship's personnel, your tour operator, and the rest of your client group. (Sometimes, engaging the survivor in the business that must be taken care of actually helps them manage.)

For the Survivor

- Assist in making the decision about the disposition of the body and relay it to the doctor or, when appropriate, the port agent. Instruct the port agent to TELEX back to the ship any flight schedules or other details arranged.

- Help assemble necessary papers (passports, insurance policy, etc.) and ensure that the valuables of the deceased are safeguarded.

- Prepare the survivor for the expenses that will be incurred and help deal with insurance. Expenses for returning home — hotels, transportation to the airport, return flight tickets — must be paid immediately in most cases. Flying the body home can cost thousands of dollars. If your client has insurance call the insurance company's 24-hour, 800 number immediately. If there is no insurance to cover these costs, the cruise line will usually advance what is needed. The surviving member will, of course, be asked to sign forms taking full responsibility for paying back the advance. When there is insurance, these problems, obviously, are simplified.

- Assist survivor in making calls or TELEXing relatives at home.

- For the survivor who wants to fly home, help with packing. (For those who opt to go home you will be leaving them in the care of port agents.)

- Should a survivor or companion want to continue the cruise but change cabins, contact the hotel manager to see what can be done.

For Ship's Personnel

As mentioned, your main tasks are to assist the ship's personnel in relating the decisions that are involved and moving the papers they require to complete the business end of a passenger's death. You do so by working with your client to make the decisions about the disposition of the body, or by contacting next of kin to make that decision and communicating it to the ship's staff. You also assist them by getting the passport of the deceased to the purser and dealing with tallying up expenses and checking insurance papers. Generally speaking, all of the things you do in support of the survivor or traveling companion will make the job of the ship's staff easier because the surviving party will have someone holding his or her hand and expediting decisions. Remember, the ship must stay on schedule during this crisis. Anything you can do to assure this matter will be greatly appreciated.

For Your Tour Operator

You will want to TELEX your tour operator immediately. Sometimes they can assist in contacting a family member. You will also be required to fill out an accident/death report (*Example 12.1*).

For the Rest of the Group

Sometimes others are a bit shaken by a death in their midst. Even if they had not become close, those who shared a table with the deceased and his or her spouse or companion will feel a sense of loss and experience some anxiety. Naturally, in some instances, the death was expected and the survivor will even be able to reassure the others that the deceased "would have wanted us all to go on and have a good time."

It is up to you to sense where your clients are emotionally and to invite them to talk to you privately if they need to. Whether a spouse, family member, traveling companion or simply a tour-mate, bear in mind that people (men, especially) often cover up their feelings in such situations, and that each of us is different — some people need to talk, some to be diverted and others to be left alone.

ACCIDENT/DEATH REPORT

Passenger Name _____   Phone _____

Address _____

City _____   State _____   Zip _____

REPORT

Date of Injury _____   Time of Injury _____

Where did the accident occur? _____

On Board   Y ☐   N ☐   (If yes) Location _____

Did accident occur during rough seas?   Y ☐   N ☐

In Port   Y ☐   N ☐   (If yes) Port City _____

How did accident occur? (state facts not opinions.)

_____

_____

_____

_____

Part of body affected _____

What action was taken? _____

_____

_____

_____

Was patient hospitalized?   Y ☐   N ☐

(If yes) Name of Hospital _____   Doctor _____

Did passenger have medical insurance?   Y ☐   N ☐

Was insurance company notified at time of injury? Y ☐   N ☐

Was passenger able to continue the cruise?   Y ☐   N ☐

(If no) How did they return home?   Date _____

IN CASE OF DEATH

Who notified the cruise host? _____

Date of notification _____   Time of notification _____

What action did you take? _____

_____

_____

_____

Cruise Host Signature _____   Date _____

Tour Code _____   Ship _____

Example 12.1 Accident/Death Report

part III

end of trip

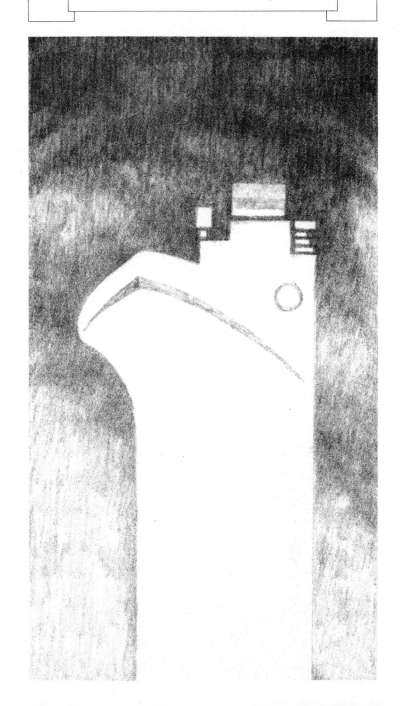

Chapter 13

Final Disembarkation

Each ship has its own system for disembarking its passengers at the end of a cruise. The ship's staff will always hold a disembarkation talk to inform all passengers of their procedures, which vary depending on the country, port, flight schedules and world situations. Even if you think you know their procedure, check with the ship's staff at the beginning of the cruise before talking with your own group.

Final Disembarkation Briefing

You should hold this briefing soon after the ship's disembarkation talk. If you let the ship's staff know you want to meet with your group immediately after their talk, they will make the announcement following their briefing, specifying the area where your clients are to meet with you. Your main purpose is to go over all information about disembarkation, flight schedules, customs and luggage procedures to make sure it is clear.

Because the ship's briefing will have covered return flights for all passengers on board, by the time clients get to you they may have a case of information overload. Sometimes staff will say, "If you have an early flight, you will disembark first." Be assured you will always have a question like, "How do I know if I have an early flight?" Common also are questions about customs, some as silly as "Do we have to declare liquor if we bought a bottle on board and drank it during the cruise?" The fact is that by the end of the cruise people are tired of travel, food and time changes. They are wondering how they are going to get all their purchases packed and home safely. They have been briefed about many details unfamiliar to them. They have a hard time visualizing and remembering. (Many are also just plain hard of hearing.)

So be sure to save time in your briefing to answer their questions — and, again, be prepared for humorous questions. One famous one is, "Do I put my suitcase outside my cabin door before or after I go to bed?" A passenger service representative was once asked, "Do I put the luggage tag on the outside or the inside of my suitcase?" Answer them with a smile.

If you understand the ship's disembarkation procedures, you'll be able to explain the ins and outs to your group. To be able to respond to their concerns, you need to be aware of the following procedures.

Flight Schedules: Flight schedules are one of the most important items that determine when passengers disembark. In this regard, the cruise line has many kinds of passengers to deal with:

- Cruise-only passengers, also known as independents, who have made their own flight reservations and are responsible for getting themselves to the airport at their own expense
- Charter passengers, who were booked on a charter flight through the cruise line but are still considered air/sea passengers
- Air/sea passengers who were booked on regularly scheduled airline flights through the cruise line

Return Flight Information: On many ships, toward the middle of the cruise all passengers will be asked to provide return flight information along with their airline tickets. The ship's staff will provide all passengers with a printed envelope they are to complete. Information and directions for doing so may be printed on a separate form attached to the envelope. Passengers often feel concerned about "giving up" their airline tickets. It is important that you tell your clients ahead of time about the entire procedure (you may have done this at your initial briefing.) You must fully explain to them why the cruise line needs the tickets and assure them that their tickets are safe.

The cruise line needs this information to:

- Reconfirm flights
- Assign seats
- Get baggage tags
- Tag baggage to the final destination
- Confirm smoking/nonsmoking, window/middle/aisle seats
- Sometimes pull tickets and give them to the airlines ahead of time
- Arrange for passenger requests such as wheelchairs or special meals

Cruise line staff then confirm all flights and sometimes obtain airline baggage tags. (With increasing concerns about security, boarding passes are becoming harder to obtain ahead of time. In most cases, the seats will be confirmed but boarding passes will be issued at the airport.) *Example 13.1* is a Royal Cruise Lines letter with instructions for filling out the Air/Sea Ticket Envelope (*Example 13.2*).

Dear Cruise Guest,

Although you have only just arrived on board the Golden Odyssey, we must turn your thoughts for a moment toward your disembarkation on October 12. Please identify the group below which describes your travel plans following this cruise. Return any requested information/air tickets to the Cruise Office, Deck 6, by **12:00 noon, Sunday, October 1.**

• •

A. *BRITISH AIRWAYS FLIGHT #1631 ("OPEN") TO LONDON - OCTOBER 12*

Passengers flying from Athens to London's Heathrow Airport on October 12 on British Airways #1631 (may be marked "Open" on your air ticket). *This includes passengers continuing to the U.S./Canada on October 12 and those on Royal Cruise Line's "London Showtime" 2-day post-cruise program.*

1. Please fill out the attached "Air/Sea" envelope.
2. Enclose all airline tickets for your return flight(s) on October 12, <u>both</u> the B.A. flight to London and any onward connections you may have. Airline tickets will be returned to you later in the cruise.
   London Showtime passengers: Please also include air tickets for your return flight(s) on October 14 from London.
3. Return completed Air/Sea envelope with airline tickets to the Cruise Office by <u>12:00 noon, Sunday, October 1.</u>

- -

B. *PASSENGERS FLYING FROM ATHENS ON OCTOBER 12 ON:*
   - *Pan Am #61 to Frankfurt*
   - *TWA #851 to Kennedy Airport, New York*
   - *KLM #506 to Amsterdam*

1. Please fill out the attached "Air/Sea" envelope.
2. Enclose all return airline tickets for flights. *on October 12 only*, including the flight from Athens and any connecting flights you may have.
3. Return completed Air/Sea envelope with airline tickets to the Cruise Office by <u>12:00 noon Sunday, October 1.</u>

- -

C. *OTHER PASSENGERS ("INDEPENDENTS") DISEMBARKING IN PIRAEUS ON OCTOBER 12*

Passengers who are not on any of the above-mentioned flights, i.e. those staying in Athens after the cruise <u>or</u> flying on October 12 on flights *other than* those listed above.

1. Please complete the information below and return to the Cruise Office no later than <u>12:00 noon Sunday, October 1.</u>
2. Royal Cruise Line is pleased to reconfirm all flights from Athens for **Independent Passengers departing October 12, 13 or 14** *only*. Flights after October 14, or those originating in cities other than Athens, must be reconfirmed after your arrival in Athens or the city in which your flight originates.

Name(s)_____   Stateroom _____

Flight Date _____   Airline/Flight # _____

From _____   To _____
               (city)   (city)

Example 13.1 Air/Sea Instruction Letter

Royal Cruise Line

Air/Sea Cruises

IMPORTANT

Simplified check-in system for Air/Sea passengers ONLY

Please complete all information requested below and return to the Cruise Office.

1. Name(s) _____ Stateroom No. _____
   (Last name first, please)
2. Airline _____ Flight Number _____ Date of Flight _____
3. Final flight destination of your airline ticket _____
4. Total airline baggage tags you need for your CHECKED luggage only _____
   (Number)
5. Seating: Smoking _____ or Non-Smoking _____
6. If possible, I (we) wish to sit with _____
7. Please check to make sure you have enclosed your airline tickets _____
   (Check)
8. Are you taking a post-cruise program? _____ Yes _____ No
9. Please list hotel assignment noted on your steamship ticket _____

===================== FOR YOUR INFORMATION =====================

This envelope will be returned to you prior to departure. Enclosed will be your remaining Flight Coupons and your Baggage Tags.
IMPORTANT – Please do not pack any of these documents. You will need all of them to board the aircraft.

Example 13.2 Air/Sea Ticket Envelope

Disembarkation Procedures: As a general rule, when disembarkation is by flight, passengers are called by flight departure times. Those with the earliest flights disembark first. Independent passengers (the ones who have handled their own flights) disembark last, unless they, too, booked an early return flight. When there is sufficient time for all passengers to meet connecting flights, disembarkation may proceed by deck. As each deck is called, passengers will be asked to surrender their embarkation cards (*Example 6.1*) so that deck and cabin numbers can be confirmed as they leave the ship.

Baggage Handling

After collecting all the tickets and return flight information, the staff will confirm the flights and either request seating from the airline or seat the plane themselves. The tickets will be returned to each passenger along with both airline (if available) and cruise line baggage tags. The number of baggage tags will correspond to the number of checked bags your client has declared on the air ticket envelope. Cruise line baggage tags vary depending on how the ship disembarks its passengers, and their procedure varies depending on passenger's return flight schedules.

Most ships color-code their baggage tags (*Example 13.3*) to correspond to particular flights. They may use 5 to 10 colors, and each color may have several numbers. Below is an example of Princess Cruise Lines baggage tags showing white 2 and purple 3. The ship may have white tags from 1-6 and purple tags from 1-6. Passengers place the baggage tags on checked luggage and take the stubs. When their color and number are called, they disembark, showing the stub to the security

Example 13.3 Baggage Tags by Color

guard at the gangway. Baggage is usually placed in the disembarkation areas by color code, so if your clients have green tags, they go to the green area to find their luggage. Some cruise lines will arrange luggage alphabetically by last name within the color code.

Customs: Some dock areas have luggage carts and some have porters available. After passengers claim luggage they proceed through customs (if they are in a foreign port or have been out of the country) and exit the building. Cruise-line staff may be available to direct them to airport transportation and/or assist them in getting a taxi.

Final Briefing and Farewell Party

If you have time, hold both a final briefing and a farewell party. Not only does the farewell party have a different atmosphere from that of the briefing, but you might not have time at the party to cover all the information you need to present. In addition to responding to your clients' questions about disembarkation, here are some important points to cover:

Acknowledgements: If ship's staff attend your farewell party, make a general announcement thanking them, together and individually, if appropriate, for the wonderful job they did. If they organized something special like a galley tour, acknowledge them for that. Let your clients know the staff was responsible for a particular event. The staff will appreciate it and it will make your job easier the next time you come aboard.

Acknowledge specifically those in your group who participated in the masquerade, talent show, games or other activities you or the ship conducted. You can find out who won the ship's competitions from the cruise director's staff. If they are part of your group, announce their names and have them stand up. Also ask whether anyone won at bingo or in the casino. (Tease them that ten percent of their winnings must go to the cruise host's retirement fund!)

Client End-of-Cruise Evaluations: You already announced at your first briefing that clients were to take their sealed tour operator evaluation forms to this final briefing. Place the envelopes in a pillow case and have a staff person or a member of your group draw the winner. (Be prepared to hand out one of your prizes — maybe a bottle of wine, a photo from the cruise or a small souvenir gift that you found on a shore excursions.

If your clients are required to mail their end-of-cruise evaluations directly to the company, or if your company does not allow you to read client evaluations, you can tell your clients you would appreciate a short note indicating what they liked and disliked about your services. This information will provide you with a better understanding of passenger needs for future cruises. Ask them to comment on the usefulness of your port letters, maps and other handouts. Requesting this evaluation of your performance also serves as a reminder to them to include a gratuity to you (assuming it is your company's policy).

Luggage: Remind your passengers to place their luggage outside their cabin doors the evening before final disembarkation. All ships differ, but this is usually done between 8:00 P.M. and 3:00 A.M. Check the ship's newspaper. Remind them to leave out something to wear home the following day. (If they forget, they won't be the first ones to go to the airport in their pajamas.)

Prizes/Gifts: Give out prizes for quizzes or activities your group participated in during the cruise (see chapter 4, Preparing Handouts, and chapter 8, Hosting Group Activities).

- Pass out diplomas for crossing the equator, for being an international or first-time sailor. Remember, if they are going to another activity after the briefing or farewell party, just show them the certificates and then deliver them to their cabins. They won't want to walk around the ship carrying these papers.

- If you have purchased small (50¢ to $1.00 each) end-of-cruise gifts for your clients, now is a good time to pass them out. (Alternatively, you can use them to decorate their dining room tables on the final night.)

Chapter 14

Returning Home

In this chapter your responsibilities to your clients and to your tour operator are outlined before presenting some comments that pertain strictly to you.

For Your Clients

If you have a pre-formed group (all from the same area, all meeting at the same airport, and all traveling to the ship together), you usually accompany them on the return flight and say good-bye at the final destination. Your responsibility ends at the baggage claim area in the home city.

If those in your group are going to different cities, your responsibilities formally end after final disembarkation; however, as a professional, always be willing to help your passengers at all times. In other words, if someone has a problem on the return flight, continue to do whatever you can. If time permits, you may also want to be in the baggage claim area on the dock to assist them in finding their luggage.

For Your Tour Operator

Your tour operator should have provided you with a complimentary return airline ticket as part of the cruise package. In addition, as stated at the outset, the following expenses should have been covered by the tour operator:

- The cost of transportation to and from the airport
- Meals not provided during travel time to and from the ship
- Hotel accommodations if required for positioning
- Expenses incurred for visas required

Now is the time to start thinking about preparing the final reports your tour operator requires when you are back from the cruise. They are:

- General cruise report (*Example 14.1*)

- Personal expense report (*Example 14.2*)

- Cruise expense report (*Example 14.3*)

- Problem passengers report (*Example 2.3*)

- Accident and death reports, if applicable (*Example 12.1*)

You need to send these reports along with the clients' end-of-cruise evaluations (*Example 2.5*) to your tour operator. Most tour operators do not send your final pay and expense reimbursement check until they have received all reports and paperwork and have completed their audit.

For Yourself

I strongly advise you to keep records for your future tours. This information will be invaluable the next time you board that ship or visit that destination. If you have a computer, the task is relatively easy:

- Keep notes on what you learn about each ship you work on, who the important people are, and what they do.

- Review and update your briefing notes and port information soon after a cruise, eliminating whatever did not work.

- Keep maps and specific notes on what did work.

- Read your clients' evaluations carefully (assuming your tour operator passes them on to you). Most evaluations contain constructive criticism, so try not to be defensive. Anything that alerts you to ways of making your clients' trip more enjoyable is bound to make your job easier.

GENERAL CRUISE REPORT

Cruise Host Name_____   Tour # _____

Cruise Line_____   Pax # _____

Ship _____   Embarkation _____

Sailing Date _____   Disembarkation _____

SHIP	**Excellent**	**Good**	**Fair**	**Poor**
Dining room service				
Food quality				
Cabin service				
Cabin cleanliness				
Quality of entertainment				
Ship's activities				
Weather on the cruise				
Overall cleanliness of ship				
Overall atmosphere of cruise				

Does the ship have handicap facilities? (Describe)

CONTACTS	**Name**	**Makes arrangements for**
Captain		
Cruise Director		
Bar Manager		
Shore Excursion Manager		
Purser		
Maitre d'		
Hotel Manager		
Passenger Service Rep		

(Note other appropriate personnel to contact for cocktail parties, office hours, galley tour, cabin changes, etc)

FUNCTION LOCATIONS: Note locations and capacities for functions: (Cocktail parties, briefings, office hours)

FUNCTION	**Location**	**Capacity**	**Time**
Initial Briefing			
Final Briefing			
Welcome Cocktail Party			
Farewell Cocktail Party			
Office Hours			

Example 14.1 General Cruise Report

SHORE EXCURSIONS:
(Please answer the following questions Yes or No.

Were they value for the money?   Yes ☐   No ☐

Were coaches and guides acceptable?   Yes ☐   No ☐

Were there any physical restrictions?   Yes ☐   No ☐

(If yes, please describe) _____

_____

PROBLEMS — List below any problems you encountered with:

Ship's Staff: _____

_____

_____

Ship's Facilities: _____

_____

_____

Passengers: _____

_____

_____

Suggestions for improvements in the service we provide to our clients:

_____

_____

_____

SUMMARY OF THE CRUISE

_____

_____

_____

_____

_____

_____

_____

_____

_____

Example 14.1 General Cruise Report

CRUISE HOST PERSONAL EXPENSE REPORT

Cruise Host Name _____   Tour Date _____

Cruise Name _____   Tour Code _____

Date	Description	Amount

_____   Visa   _____
_____   Transportation to Airport   _____

POSITIONING
_____   Transfer to Hotel   _____
_____   Hotel   _____
_____   Meals   _____

_____   Transfer to Cruise Ship   _____
_____   Laundry _____ days X $3.00=   _____

Miscellaneous:

_____   _____   _____
_____   _____   _____
_____   _____   _____

_____   Transfer Ship to Airport   _____
_____   Transfer Airport to Home   _____

_____   Total Personal Expenses   _____

Example 14.2 Personal Expense Report

CRUISE EXPENSE REPORT

Ship _____   Cruise Date _____

Destination _____   Tour Code _____

Cruise Host _____   # Days   14   # Pax 40

SCHEDULED EXPENSES - TIPS   Estimated   Actual

Maitre d' (for group) $1.00 pp x _____ pax =   _____

Head Waiter (self only) $5.00 $5.00   _____

Cabin Steward (self only) $3.00 per day x _____ days = $42.00   _____

Waiter (self only) $3.00 per day x _____ days = $42.00   _____

Busboy (self only) $1.50 per day x _____ days = $21.00   _____

Bartender for cocktail party $10.00 $10.00   _____

Waiters for cocktail party 3 x $5 each = $15.00   _____

UNSCHEDULED EXPENSES

Emergency fund $1.00 pp per day x 14 days $560.00   _____

MISCELLANEOUS EXPENSES — Please describe below.

(Birthday/Anniversary/Phone/Telex)

_____

_____

_____

_____

_____

_____

_____

_____

Total Expense Advance   minus   _____

Total Scheduled Expense   minus   _____

Total Unscheduled Expense   minus   _____

Total Personal Expense   minus   _____

Total Due Cruise Host/Travel Time Tours   _____

(Circle appropriate one)

Example 14.3 Cruise Expense Report

Conclusion

Now that you have been introduced to this exciting profession, and learned about the various functions you are expected to perform, it is up to you to take it on as your own. Each person is different and each cruise host will shape the job according to her or his unique personality and special talents.

Just as cruise hosts are different from each other, so are the groups you will be leading. Be flexible and experiment. Don't feel you must try everything on your first cruise. Remember, if you are bogged down with paperwork and not spending time with your group, you will miss the real point of this book and the real satisfaction that comes with cruise hosting.

For those ready to advance to the next level, you might want to know about the special training available at International Tour Management Institute, Inc. Although some colleges have isolated courses in the field of travel, ITMI is the only school in the United States that teaches cruise hosting as a profession and provides its graduates with job placement assistance. More information about ITMI is in the appendix.

Finally, I would be happy to hear about your adventures, and to receive suggestions based on your experiences at sea. The more we share our knowledge and skills, the more indispensable we become to the travel agencies and the cruise lines with which we hope to develop ongoing relationships. You may write to me, Brooke Bravos, at: P.O. Box 233, Sausalito, California 94966.

Glossary and Excerpts
from CLIA Manual

A special thanks to
Cruise Lines International Association
for permitting me to reproduce
portions of their manual
(pages 175 through 186)

GLOSSARY OF BOOKING TERMS

ACCOMMODATION — (See Room)

ADD ON — A supplementary charge added to the cruise fare, usually applied to correlated air fare and/or post cruise land tours.

AFT — Near, toward or in the rear (stern) of the ship.

AIR/SEA — A package consisting of the two forms of travel, i.e., air to and from the port of embarkation as well as the cruise itself.

BAGGAGE ALLOWANCE — That amount of baggage, generally consisting of the passenger's personal effects, carried by the cruise line free of charge.

BASIS TWO — The cabin rate *per person* applicable to a cabin capable of accommodating at least two persons. Also referred to as double occupancy.

BOOKING — A telephone request to a line's reservtions department to secure an option on a cabin.

CABIN — (See Room)

CATEGORY — A price gradient of similar cabins from the most expensive to the least expensive, or vice versa.

CLASS — Extinct on most cruises. On some trans-ocean voyages denotes an overall level of ambience and cost, such as "First Class", "Tourist Class" or "Transatlantic Class." Cruises are generally termed: one-class service.

CONDUCTOR'S TICKET — A free cruise ticket usually associated with groups of passengers traveling together, the entitlement to which is governed by each Line's policy.

CRUISE FARE — The actual cost of the cruise excluding all extras such as taxes, port charges, airfare, gratutities and the like.

DEBARKATION — Exiting from the ship.

DECK CHAIR — Open deck chaise lounge which is generally provided on a complimentary basis.

DECK PLAN — An overhead diagram illustrating cabin and public room locations in relation to each other.

DEPOSIT — A part payment of the cruise fare required at the time of booking to secure the cabin being reserved.

EMBARKATION — Entering or boarding the ship.

FORWARD — Toward the fore or bow (front) of the ship.

FINAL PAYMENT — Payment of the full cruise fare plus any necessary or agreed extras, such as taxes, air add on, preparatory to issuance of correlated travel documents.

FIRST SITTING — The earlier of two meal times in the ship's dining room.

FLY/CRUISE — (See Air/Sea)

GRATUITIES — The passenger's personal expression of thanks (tips) to the ship's service personnel for services received.

GRT — Gross registered tonnage, i.e., a measurement of 100 cubic feet of enclosed revenue earning space within a ship. (See Space Ratio)

GUARANTEE — The cruise line's promise that the passenger will sail on a stated voyage in a specified price catagory or type of cabin, at an agreed rate no higher than would ordinarily apply for that voyage, which *may* result in an improvement of accommodations at no additional cost.

GUARANTEE SHARE FARE — Acceptance by some lines of a single booking at the cost-saving double occupancy rate, with the understanding that the client is willing to share use of the cabin with a stranger of the same sex.

INSIDE — A cabin having no windows or portholes to offer a view of the sea, or of the river.

LOWER BED — A single bed placed at the conventional height from the floor.

MIDSHIPS — In or toward the middle of the ship; the longitudinal center portion of the ship.

OFFER — The cruise line's commitment for accommodations then available which may be suitable to the passenger's needs or wishes.

OPEN SITTING — Free access to unoccupied tables in the ship's dining room, as opposed to specific table assignments.

OPTION — The cruise line's offering of a specific cabin (or guarantee) for a specified period of time during which the passenger decides whether or not to accept. Acceptance is confirmed either by a deposit or final payment.

OUTSIDE — A cabin having window(s) or porthole(s) offering a view of the sea, or of the river.

PASSAGE CONTRACT — Detailed terms of responsibility and accountability found in the cruise ticket.

PETS — Any ordinary domesticated bird of animal. None are carried aboard cruise voyages.

PORT — The left side of the ship when facing forward.

PORT CHARGES — An assessment which also includes port taxes, collected by the line and paid to a local government authority.

PORTHOLES — Circular "windows" in the side of the ship's hull or superstructure.

PORT TAXES — A charge levied by local government authority to be paid by the passenger. In some air/sea packages port taxes are included in the final price.

QUAD RATE — An economical per person rate available to individuals for quadruple occupancy on a guarantee share basis.

REVIEW DATES — A periodic evaluation of the progress of the sale and promotion of a group combined with attendant cabin utilization.

ROOM — The passenger's room, stateroom or personal accommodation.

SAILING TIME — The actual hour at which the ship is scheduled to clear the dock and sail.

SECOND SITTING — The later of two meal times in the ship's dining room.

SHARE BASIS — (See Guarantee Share Fare)

SHORE EXCURSIONS — Off-the-ship tours at ports of call for which an extra charge is usually applied.

SINGLE OCCUPANCY — Sole occupancy of a cabin which is designed to accommodate two or more passengers in which instance a premium is ordinarily charged.

SPACE RATIO — A measurement of cubic space per passenger. Gross Registered Tonnage divided by number of passengers (double occupancy) equals Space Ratio. (rounded to nearest whole number)

STARBOARD — The right side of the ship facing forward.

STATEROOM — (See Room)

STOPOVER — Leaving the ship at a port of call and rejoining it at a subsequent port of call or upon the ship's return to the earlier port of call.

TENDER — A smaller vessel, sometimes the ship's lifeboat, used to move passengers to and from the ship and shore when the ship is at anchor.

TBA — To be assigned.

TRANSFERS — Conveyances between the ship and other modes such as airports, hotels or departure points for shore excursions.

TRIPLE RATE — An economical per person rate available to individuals for triple occupancy on a guarantee share-fare basis.

TYPE — (See Category)

UPPER BED — A single size bed higher from the floor than usual (similar to a bunk bed) often recessed into the ceiling or wall by day.

WAITLIST — Not a guarantee, but the cruise line's endeavor to obtain accommodations for passengers on a first-come-first-served basis when all cabins are presently either sold, under deposit or under option.

GLOSSARY OF NAUTICAL TERMS

ABEAM — Off the side of the ship, at a right angle to length of the ship.

ACCOMMODATION LADDER — External folding stairway for access from ashore or from a tender along side.

AFT — Near, toward or in the rear (stern) of the ship.

ALLEYWAY — A passageway or corridor.

ALOFT — Above the superstructure; in, at or near the masthead.

AMIDSHIPS — In or toward the middle of the ship; the longitudinal center portion of the ship.

ASTERN — Abaft; or beyond the ship's stern.

ATHWARTSHIPS — Across the ship from side to side.

BACKWASH — Motion in the water caused by the propeller(s) moving in a reverse (astern) direction.

BAR — Sandbar, usually caused by tidal or current conditions near the shore.

BATTEN DOWN— To secure all open hatches or equipment for worthiness while under way.

BEAM — Width of the ship (amidships) between the widest point of its two sides.

BEARING — Compass direction, usually expressed in degrees, from the ship to a particular destination or objective.

BELLS — Audible sounding of ship's time — one bell for each progressive half hour to a total of eight, commencing at half past the hours of 4, 8, and 12.

BERTH — Dock, pier or quay (key).

BERTH — The bed or beds within the passengers' cabins.

BILGE — Lowermost spaces of the ship's innerstructure.

BINNACLE — The ship's compass.

BOW — Front or forward portion of the ship.

BRIDGE — Navigational and command control center of the ship.

BULKHEAD — Upright partition (wall) dividing the ship into cabins or compartments.

BULWARK — The side of the ship at or near the main deck.

CAPSTAN — Vertically mounted motor driven spindle used to wind in hawsers or cables.

CLEAT — Horizontal wedge-shaped device to which hawsers or cables are made fast.

COAMING — Raised partition around hatches or between doorways to prevent water from entering.

COLORS — A national flag or ensign flown from the mast or stern post.

COMPANIONWAY — Interior stairway.

CONNING — To superintend the steering of a ship.

COURSE — Direction in which the ship is headed, usually expressed in compass degrees.

CROW'S NEST — Partially enclosed platform at the top of the mast used by a lookout.

DAVIT — A device for raising and lowering the ship's lifeboats.

DEADLIGHT — A ventilated porthole cover through which light cannot be emitted.

DOCK — Berth, pier or quay (key).

DRAFT — Measurement in feet from waterline to lowest point of ship's keel.

DRAFT NUMBERS — Located at the bow and the stern to measure draft. Numerals are 6″ high and 6″ apart.

EVEN KEEL — The ship in a true vertical position with respect to its vertical axis.

FANTAIL — The rear or aft overhang of the ship.

FATHOM — Measurement of distance equal to 6 feet.

FENDER — Anything serving as a cushion between the side of the ship and the dock or other craft.

FORE — The forward mast or the front (bow) of the ship.

FORWARD — Toward the fore or bow of the ship.

FREEBOARD — That outer part of the ship's hull between the waterline and the main deck.

FREE PORT — A port or place free of customs duty and most customs regulations.

FUNNEL — The smokestack or "chimney" of the ship.

GALLEY — The ship's kitchen.

GANGWAY — The opening through the ship's bulwarks (or thru the ship's side) and the ramp by which passengers embark and disembark.

GROSS REGISTERED TON — A measurement of 100 cubic feet of enclosed revenue earning space within a ship. (see Space Ratio)

HATCH — The covering over an opening in the ship's deck, usually of conisderable size leading to a hold.

HAWSE PIPE — Large pipe(s) in the bow of the ship thru which passes the anchor chain or hawser.

HAWSER — A rope of sufficient size and strength to tow or secure a ship.

HELM — Commonly the ship's steering wheel, but more correctly the entire steering apparatus consisting of the wheel, the rudder and their connecting cables or hydraulic systems.

HOLD — Interior space(s) below the main deck for stowage of cargo.

HOUSE FLAG — The flag which donotes the company to which the ship belongs.

HULL — The frame and body (shell) of the ship exclusive of masts, superstructure, or rigging.

INBOARD — Toward the centerline of the ship.

JACOB'S LADDER — A rope ladder usualy with wooden rungs.

KEEL — A longitudinal member extending from stem to stern at the bottom center of the ship from which all vertical framing rises.

KING POST — Vertical posts, usually in pairs, to which the ship's cargo cranes are attached.

KNOT — A unit of speed equal to one nautical mile per hour (6080.2 feet) as compared to a land mile of 5,280 feet.

LATITUDE — Angular distance measured in degrees north or south of the equator. One degree approximates 60 nautical miles.

LEAGUE — A measure of distance approximating 3.45 nautical miles.

LEEWARD — (Pronounced - Lew-ard) — In the direction of that side of the ship opposite from which the wind blows.

LINE — Any rope smaller than a hawser.

LONGITUDE — Angular distance measured in degrees east or west of the prime meridian of Greenwich, England. Due to the earth's curvature, one degree of longitude will vary from approximately 60 nautical miles at the equator to zero at the north and south poles.

MANIFEST — A list or invoice of a ship's passengers, crew and cargo.

MIDSHIPS — (See Amidships)

MOOR — To secure a ship to a fixed place by hawsers, cables or anchor.

NAUTICAL MILE — 6,080.2 feet, as compared to a land mile of 5,280 feet.

OUTBOARD — Away from the centerline of the ship, whether toward the ship's sides or beyond them.

PADDLEWHEEL — A wheel with boards around its circumference, and, commonly, the sole source of propulsion for riverboats.

PITCH — The alternate rise and fall of a ship's bow which may occur when underway.

PLIMSOLL MARK — One of a series of load lines marked on the side of a ship at the waterline to prevent overloading.

PORT — The left side of the ship when facing forward toward the bow.

PROW — The bow or the stem (the front) of the ship.

QUAY — (Pronounced - key) A dock, berth or pier.

REGISTRY — The country under whose laws the ship and its owners are obliged to comply, in addition to compliance with the laws of the countries at which the ship calls and/or embarks/disembarks passengers/cargo.

RIGGING — The ropes, chains, cables and the like which support the ship's masts, spars, kingposts, cranes and the like.

ROLL — The alternate sway of a ship from side to side which may occur when underway.

RUDDER — That fin-like device astern and below the waterline which when turned to port or starboard will cause the bow of the ship to respond with a similar turn.

RUNNING LIGHTS — Three lights (green on the starboard side, red on the portside and white at the top of the mast) required by international law to be lighted when the ship is in motion between sunset and sunrise.

SCREW — The ship's propeller.

SCUPPER — An opening in the bulwarks of a ship through which water accumulated on deck can flow freely overboard.

SOUNDING — Determining the depth of the water either by a weighted rope soundline in shallow waters or by electronic echo in deep waters.

SPACE RATIO — A measurement of cubic space per passenger. Gross Registered Tonnage divided by number of passengers (basis two) equals Space Ratio (rounded to nearest whole number).

STABILIZERS — A gyroscopically operated fin-like device extending from both sides of the ship below the waterline to provide a more stable motion.

STACK — The funnel or "chimney" from which the ship's gasses of combustion are freed to the atmosphere.

STAGE — the gangway of a paddlewheel steamboat.

STARBOARD — Right side of the ship when facing forward toward the bow.

STEERAGEWAY — A rate of foward or reverse motion necessary to allow the ship to "answer" a repositioning of the rudder (helm).

STEM — The extreme bow or prow of the ship.

STERN —The extreme rear of the ship, or toward the rear.

STOW — To fill or load a ship with cargo or provisions.

SUPERSTRUCTURE — The structural part of the ship above the maindeck.

TENDER — A smaller vessel, sometimes the ship's lifeboat, used to move passengers to and from the ship and shore when the ship is at anchor.

WAKE — The track of agitated water left behind a ship in motion.

WATERLINE — The line at the side of the ship's hull which corresponds with the surface of the water.

WEATHER SIDE — That side of the ship exposed to the wind or to the weather.

WEIGH — to raise, e.g., to "weigh" the anchor.

WINCH — Usually a power operated machine with a horizontal spindle used to operate the ship's cranes and/or davits.

WINDWARD — Toward the wind, to the direction from which the wind blows.

YAW — To erratically deviate from the ship's course, usually caused by heavy seas.

DS — Diesel ship

MS — Motor ship

MTS — Motor turbine ship

MV — Motor vessel

NS — Nuclear ship

RHMS — Royal Hellenic Mail Ship (old)

RMS — Royal Mail Ship

SS — Steamship

STR — Steamer

TS — Twin Screw

TSS — Turbine steamship

USS — United States Ship (U.S. Navy)

NAME: M.S. GOLDEN ODYSSEY
COMPANY: ROYAL CRUISE LINE
ORIGINALLY BUILT: 1974
COUNTRY OF REGISTRY: BAHAMAS
SPEED: 22.5 KNOTS
NORMAL CREW SIZE: 200
NATIONALITY OF CREW
    OFFICERS: GREEK
    HOTEL STAFF: GREEK
    CRUISE STAFF: INTERNATIONAL

SIZE CAPACITY

GROSS REGISTERED TONNAGE: 10,500
LENGTH: 427 FEET   **BEAM:** 63 FEET
TOTAL CAPACITY: (Incl. uppers): 509
NORMAL SHORT CRUISE CAP. (Basis 2) 460
NORMAL LONG CRUISE CAP. (Basis 2) 460
SPACE RATIO: 23

ACCOMMODATIONS

TYPE	No. Outside	No. Inside
SUITES	8	
W/ 2 LOWERS	167	31
UPPER & LOWER	16	15
TOTAL	191	46
TOTAL CABINS	237	

PUBLIC ROOM CAPACITIES

NAME	Capacity
WOODEN HORSE, BAR	32
CALYPSO BAR	85
BELLEVUE BAR	6
CARD ROOM	36
LOTUS RESTAURANT	252
CALYPSO LOUNGE/DISCO . . . . ;	85
LIBRARY/WRITING ROOM	16
ULYSSES LOUNGE	408
THEATRE LOUNGE/CONFERENCE RM.	154
CASINO	

Various public rooms may be used as meeting facilities.

FACILITIES

AIR COND. FULLY	MEDICAL FACILITY
AQUA PAR COURSE	PASSENGER DECKS (7)
BARBER SHOP	PHOTO/VIDEO Services
BEAUTY SALON	PING PONG
BINGO	RADIO (3 channels)
BOUTIQUE	IN ALL CABINS
ELECTRICAL CURRENT	SAUNA
(110 AC, 60 Cy./220V)	SHUFFLEBOARD
ELEVATORS (2)	STABILIZERS
FULL DECK PROMENADE	DENNY BROWN
GYMNASIUM	SWIMMING POOL
HAIR DRYERS ALLOWED	OUTSIDE
LAUNDRY/	TELEPHONES (Direct dial
Pressing Services	ship to shore)
MASSAGE	24-HOUR ROOM SERVICE
	TOUR OFFICE

OTHER USEFUL INFORMATION

No. of sittings for dinner:	2
Usual dinner hours:	6:45 p.m. and 8:30 p.m.
Dining room dress code:	Jacket and tie after 6 p.m.
Special diet & Kosher meals:	American Heart Assn. entrees.
	Kosher meals (pre-prepared)
Tipping Policy:	$8:00/per passenger/per day divided:
	$4.00 to cabin steward
	$4.00 to dining steward

m/s CROWN ODYSSEY

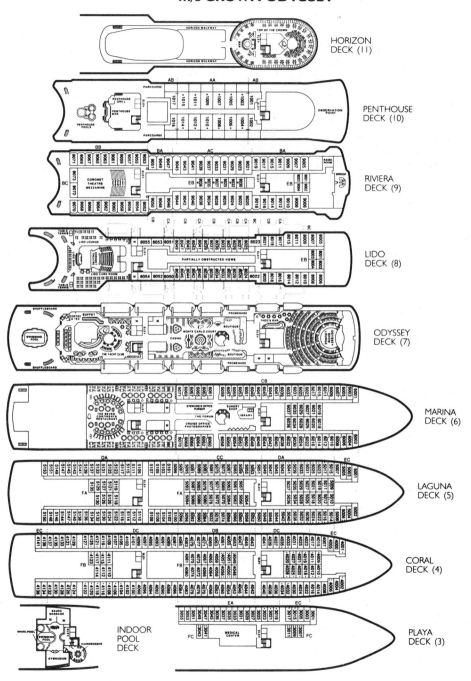

HORIZON DECK (11)

PENTHOUSE DECK (10)

RIVIERA DECK (9)

LIDO DECK (8)

ODYSSEY DECK (7)

MARINA DECK (6)

LAGUNA DECK (5)

CORAL DECK (4)

INDOOR POOL DECK

PLAYA DECK (3)

NASSAU

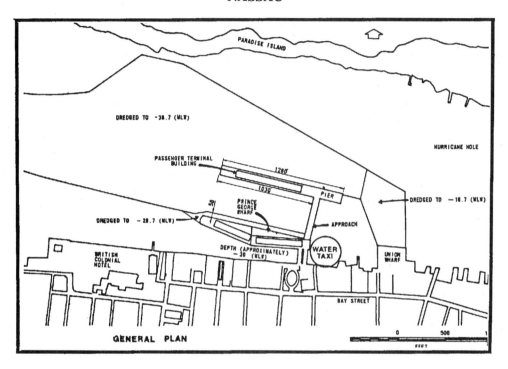

Prince George Wharf is centrally located. Bay Street, the main downtown shopping area is a mere two hundred yards away.

Upon disembarking, passengers will find taxis at their disposal marked along the pier. Water-taxis or ferry boats also provide constant transportation to Paradise Island.

Parking is available for visitors along the pier for the duration of the stay of the ships. There is no long-term parking.

Situated on the pier, for the convenience of cruise-ship passengers is a Bahamas Tourist Information Center and a Bahamas Telecommunications Center.

D I N
Pastel

Appetizers

CRAB CAKES
with Spicy Dill Sauce

MARINATED EGGPLANT
with Mozzarella Cheese

SMOKED TROUT
with Garlic Cream Cheese and Fine Herbs

Salads

ROAST DUCK SALAD
with Belgian Endives
Toasted Hazelnuts, and
Creamy Marjoram Dressing

MIXED GREENS
with Blue Cheese
Vinaigrette

SLICED TOMATOES
and Anchovies

Soups

SPLIT PEA SOUP

CHICKEN BROTH AND TORTELLINI

ICED FRESH FRUIT SOUP

To Your Heart's Content

BROILED SKINLESS BREAST OF CHICKEN
with Hot Lentil Salad

Entrees

GRILLED LAMB CHOPS
Mint Basil Pesto Sauce

BROILED SALMON
with Tarragon-Hollandaise Sauce

ROAST BREAST OF CORN-FED CHICKEN
California Brandy Sauce

ROAST SIRLOIN OF BEEF
Sauce Choron

POT ROASTED PASTA
and Fresh Vegetables

Fresh Vegetables

CREAMED SPINACH

ALMOND POTATOES

Fresh Fruits and Cheeses

Desserts

WHITE CHOCOLATE MOUSSE

BABA-AU GRANDE MARNIER

FRESH FRUIT SORBETS

HOMEMADE ICE CREAM

Beverages

FRESHLY BREWED COFFEE
Regular or Decaffeinated

IMPORTED TEA, ICED TEA, MILK

HOT CHOCOLATE

Royal Cruise Line

Member of the Confrerie De "La Chaine Des Rotisseurs"
The World's Foremost and Oldest Gourmet Society

The Odyssey Wine Cellar

Champagnes

Moët et Chandon, Dom Pérignon '90
Mumm Cuvée de René Lalou Millésimé '75
Louis Roederer Cristal '85   Veuve Cliquot Ponsardin '40
G.H. Mumm & Cie, Cordon Rouge Brut '38
Moët et Chandon, Brut Impérial '40

European Sparkling Wines

Asti Spumante (Italian) '16   Blanc de Blancs (French) '16

California Methode Champenoise

Château, St. Jean, Brut '22
Piper-Sonoma, Brut '22   Korbel, Brut '19

California White Wines

Chardonnay

Joseph Phelps '24   Acacia '22   Château St. Jean '20
Kendall-Jackson '19   Beringer '15

Fumé Blanc

Robert Mondavi '16   Kendall-Jackson, Sauvignon Blanc '14
Beringer '13

California Red Wines

Cabernet Sauvignon

Jordan '27   Robert Mondavi '17   Vichon '14

Merlot

Duckhorn Vineyards '30   Sterling '16

California Blush Wines

White Zinfandel Beringer '12   Sutter Home '12

French White Wines

Burgundy

Meursault, Château de Meursault '50   Pouilly-Fuissé '28
Chablis Premier Cru '26   Mâcon Supérieur '19

Bordeaux

Mouton Cadet '15

Loire Valley

Pouilly-Fumé '21   Sancerre '19

French Red Wines

Burgundy

Nuits-St.-Georges '30   Chassagne-Montrachet '24
Côte de Beaune-Villages '19

Bordeaux

Château Margaux '105   Saint-Emilion, Vieux '19   Mouton Cadet '14

Beaujolais

Brouilly '15   Beaujolais-Villages '12

Rhône Valley

Châteauneuf-du-Pape '20   Côtes-du-Rhône '12

Italian White Wines

Pinot Grigio, Sta. Margherita '18   Orvieto Secco, Ruffino '14
Soave Classico, Bolla '13   Verdicchio dei Castelli di Jesi '13

Italian Red Wines

Barolo, Fontanafredda '19   Chianti Classico Riserva Ducale '16
Chianti, Capsula Rossa Ruffino (1 liter flask) '15   Valpolicella, Bolla '11

German Wines

Liebfraumilch, Blue Nun '14   Johannisberg Riesling '14
Piesport, Michelsberg '13

Greek White Wines

Porto Carras '13   Santa Helena '12
Lac des Roches '10   Demestica '9

Greek Red Wines

Château Clauss '18   Kava Boutari '16
Naoussa '13   Cellar '12

Rosé Wines

Côtes de Provence (French) '11   Mateus (Portuguese) '13
Boutari (Greek) '11

Non-Alcoholic Wines

White or Red '8

All Prices in U.S. Dollars
Corkage Fee of $6 applies to Wine and Spirits not from the Odyssey Wine Cellar

Tourist Bureaus

Africa

South African Tourism Board

9841 Airport Blvd , #1524	Los Angeles CA 90045	800-782-9772

Africa South

South African Tourism Board

747 3rd Ave, 20th Floor	New York NY 10017	800-822-5368

Antigua

Antigua Dept of Tourism

610 Fifth Ave	New York NY 10020	212-541-4117
121 SE 1st St, Suite 1001	Miami FL 33131	305-381-6762

Argentina

Argentine Consulate

3550 Wilshire Blvd, # 1459	Los Angeles CA 90010	213-739-9977
12 West 56th St	New York NY 10019	212- 603-0443
20 N Clark St	Chicago IL 60602	312-263-7435/7639

Aruba

Aruba Tourist Bureau

521 5th Ave	New York NY 10175	212-246-3030
85 Grand Canal Dr, # 200	Miami FL 33144	305-267-0404

Australia

Australia Naturally -Tasmania

2121 Ave of The Stars, #1270	Los Angeles CA 90067	213-552-3010

Australian Tourism Commission

489 Fifth Ave, 31st Floor	New York NY 10017	212-687-6300
2121 Ave of the Stars, #200	Los Angeles CA 90067	213-552-1988
150 N. Michigan Ave, #2130	Chicago IL 60601	312-781-5150

Austria

Austrian National Tourist Office

500 Fifth Ave	New York NY 10110	212-944-6880
500 North Michigan Ave	Chicago IL 60611	312-644-8029
1300 Post Oak Blvd	Houston TX 77056	713-850-9999
11601 Wilshire Blvd	Los Angeles CA 90025	213-477-3332

Bahamas

Bahamas Tourist Office

150 E. 52nd St	New York NY 10022	212-758-2777
255 Alhambra Circle, #415	Coral Gables FL 33134	800-Bahamas
8600 W. Bryn Mawr Ave	Chicago IL 60631	312-693-1111
3450 Wilshire Blvd, # 208	Los Angeles CA 90010	213-385-0033
44 Montgomery Ctr, # 500	San Francisco CA 94104	415-398-5502

Barbados
Barbados Tourist Board
800 Second Ave, 17th Floor	New York NY 10017	212-986-6516
3440 Wilshire Blvd, # 1215	Los Angeles CA 90010	213-380-2198

Bermuda
Bermuda Dept of Tourism
310 Madison Ave, Rm 201	New York NY 10017	212-818-9800-1-2
#3075 Wilshire Blvd, # 601	Los Angeles CA 90010	213-388-1151
R.Wacker Bldg, 150 N. Wacker, #	Chicago IL 60606	312-782-5486
235 Peachtree St, NE, # 2008	Atlanta GA 30303	404-524-1541

Brazil
Brazilian Consulate
3810 Wilshire Blvd, # 1500	Los Angeles CA 90010	213 382-3133

Brazilian Tourism Board
551 Fifth Ave, Rm 519	New York NY 10176	212-286-9600

British
British Tourist Authority
40 West 57th St, 3rd Floor	New York NY 10019	212-581-4700
625 North Michigan Ave	Chicago IL 60611	312-787-0490
350 South Figueroa St	Los Angeles CA 90071	213-628-3525
2580 Cumberland Pky	Atlanta GA 30339	404-432-9635

Bulgaria
Bulgarian Tourist Office
41 E. 42nd St, # 606	New York NY 10017	212-573-5530

Caribbean
British Virgin Islands Tourist Board
1686 Union St	San Francisco CA 94123	415-775-0344
370 Lexington Ave #511	New York NY 10017	800-835-8530

Caribbean Tourism Assn.
20 East 46th St, 4th floor	New York NY 10017	212-682-0435

Cayman Island
Cayman Island Dept. of Tourism
420 Lexington Ave	New York NY 10170	212-682-5582
2 Memorial City Plaza, 820 Gessner	Houston TX 77024	713-461-1317
3440 Wilshire Blvd	Los Angeles CA 90016	213-738-1968
980 North Michigan Ave	Chicago IL 60611	312-944-5602
250 Catalonia Ave	Coral Gables FL 33134	305-444-6551

Columbia
Columbian Govt. Tourist Office
140 East 57th St	New York NY 10022	212-688-0151

Costa Rica

Costa Rica Tourist Board

1101 Brickell Ave, #801	Miami FL 33131	800-327-7033

Curacao

Curacao Tourist Board

400 Madison Ave, # 311	New York NY 10017	212-751-8266
330 Biscayne Blvd, #808	Miami FL 33132	800-445-8266

Czechoslovakia

Czechoslovak Travel Bureau

10 East 40th St, # 1902	New York NY 10016	212-689-9720

Denmark

Danish Tourist Board

655 Third Ave	New York NY 10017	212-949-2333

Egypt

Egyptian Tourist Authority

323 Geary St, #303	San Francisco CA 94102	415-781-7676
630 Fifth Ave	New York NY 10111	212-246-6960
645 N. Michigan, #829	Chicago IL 60611	312-280-4666
5858 West Heimer, #307	Houston TX 77057	713-782-9110

Europe

European Travel Commission

630 Fifth Ave, # 610	New York NY 10111

Fiji

Fiji Visitors Bureau

5777 West Century Blvd, #220	Los Angeles CA 90045	213 568-1616

Fiji Mission to the United Nations

1 United Nations Plaza, 26th Floor	New York NY 10017	212-355-7316

Finland

Finnish Tourist Board

655 Third Ave	New York NY 10017	212-949-2333

France

French Govt. Tourist Office

610 Fifth Ave	New York NY 10020	212-315-0888
645 North Michigan Ave	Chicago IL 60611	312-337-6301
2305 Cedar Springs Rd	Dallas TX 75201	214-720-4010
9454 Wilshire Blvd, # 303	Beverly Hills CA 90212	213-271-6665

French West Indies

French West Indies

See French Govt. Tourist Office

Germany
German National Tourist Office
747 Third Ave	New York NY 10017	212-308-3300
444 South Flower St	Los Angeles CA 90071	213-688-7332

Greece
Greek National Tourist Org.
611 West 6th Street, # 2198	Los Angeles CA 90017	213-626-6696
645 Fifth Ave	New York NY 10022	212-421-5777
168 North Michigan	Chicago IL 60601	312-782-1084

Haiti
Haiti Govt. Tourist Bureau
630 Fifth Ave, # 2109	New York NY 10020	212-757-3517

Holland
Netherlands Board of Tourism
90 New Montgomery, #305	San Francisco CA 94105	213-678-8802
355 Lexington Ave, 21st Floor	New York NY 10017	213-370-7360
225 North Michigan Ave, #326	Chicago IL 60601	312-819-0300

Hong Kong
Hong Kong Tourist Assoc.
10940 Wilshire Blvd, #1220	Los Angeles CA 90024	213-208-4582
(This # will reach LA office)	San Francisco CA	415-781-4582
333 N. Michigan Ave, # 2400	Chicago IL 60601	312-782-3872
590 5th Ave, 5th Floor	New York NY 10036	212-869-5008/9

Tourist Association
590 5th Avenue, 5th Floor	New York NY 10036	212-869-5008 or 5009

India
Indian Govt. Tourist Office
30 Rockefeller Plaza	New York NY 10112	212-586-4901
3550 Wilshire #204	Los Angeles CA 90010	213-380-8855

Indonesia
Indonesian Tourist Board
3457 Wilshire	Los Angeles CA 90010	213-387-2078

Ireland
Irish Tourist Board
757 3rd Ave, 19th Floor	New York NY 10017	212-418-0800

Israel
Israel Govt. Tourist Office
350 Fifth Ave	New York NY 10118	212-560-0650
6380 Wilshire Blvd, #1700	Los Angeles CA 90048	213-658-7462
5 South Wabash Ave	Chicago IL 60603	312-782-4306

Italy
Italian Govt. Travel Office

360 Post St, #801	San Francisco CA 94108	415-392-6206
630 Fifth Ave, Rockefeller Ctr, #1565	New York NY 10111	212-245-4822
500 North Michigan Ave	Chicago IL 60611	312-644-0990

Jamacia
Jamacia Tourist Board

866 2nd Ave, 10th Floor	New York NY 10017	212-688-7650
1320 South Dixie Hwy	Coral Gables FL 33146	305-665-0557
36 S. Wabash Ave, # 1210	Chicago IL 60603	312-346-1546
3440 Wilshire Blvd, # 1207	Los Angeles CA 90010	213-384-1123
8214 Westchester, # 500	Dallas TX 75225	214-361-8778
300 West Wienca Rd, # 100A NE	Atlanta GA 30342	404-250-9971/2

Japan
Japan National Tourist Information

360 Post St, Rm 601	San Francisco CA 94108	415-989-7140
Rockefeller Plaza, 630 Fifth Ave	New York NY 10111	212-757-5640
401 North Michigan Ave	Chicago IL 60611	312-222-0874
2121 San Jacinto St, # 980	Dallas TX 75201	214-754-1820
624 South Grand Ave	Los Angeles CA 90017	213-623-1952

Kenya
Kenya Tourist Office

424 Madison Ave	New York NY 10017	212-486-1300

Korea
Korea Tourism

460 Park Ave	New York NY 10022	212-688-7543

Malaysia
Malaysian Tourist Info. Center

818 West 7th St	Los Angeles CA 90017	213-689-9702

Malta
Malta Consulate

249 East 35th St	New York NY 10016	212-725-2345

Mexico
Mexican Govt. Tourism Office

70 East Lake St, #1413	Chicago IL 60601	312-565-2786
405 Park Ave & 54th, Rm 1002	New York NY 10022	800-262-8900
128 Aragon Ave	Coral Gables FL 33134	305-443-9160
2707 N. Loop West, #450	Houston TX 77008	713-880-5153

Mexico

Mexico Govt. Tourist Office

10100 Santa Monica Blvd, #224	Los Angeles CA 90067	213-203-9335

Netherlands

Netherlands Nat Board of Tourism

355 Lexington Ave, 21st Floor	New York NY 10017	212-370-7367
90 Montgomery St	San Francisco CA 94105	415-543-6772
225 North Michigan, #326	Chicago IL 60601	312-819-0300

New Zealand

New Zealand Tourism Office

501 Santa Monica Blvd, #300	Los Angeles CA 90401	800-388-5494

New Zealand Travel Comm.

630 Fifth Ave, # 530	New York NY 10111	212-586-0060

Norway

Norwegian Consulate

2 Embarcadero Ctr, #2930	San Francisco CA 94111	415-986-0766

Norwegian Tourist Board

655 Third Ave	New York NY 10017	212-949-2333

Norwegian Information Service

825 3rd Ave	New York NY 10022	212-421-7333

Philippine

Philippine Tourism

556 Fifth Ave	New York NY 10036	212-575-7915
447 Sutter St, 5th Floor	San Francisco CA 94108	415-433-6666
3660 Wilshire Blvd, #216	Los Angeles CA 90010	213-487-4527

Portugal

Portuguese Nat Tourist Office

590 Fifth Ave	New York NY 10036	212-354-4403

Puerto Rico

Puerto Rico Tourism Co.

575 5th Ave	New York NY 10017	212-599-6262
3575 West Cahuenga Blvd, # 560	Los Angeles CA 90068	213-874-5991
200 SE 1st St, #1000	Miami FL 33131	305-381-8915

Quebec

Quebec Govt. House

17 West 50th St	New York NY 10020	212-397-0200

Tourism Quebec

P.O. Box 20000	Quebec Canada GIK 7X2	800-363-7777

Scandanavia
Scandinavia Tourist Board

8929 Wilshire Blvd, #212	Beverly Hills CA 90211	213-657-4808
655 3rd Ave	New York NY 10017	212-949-2333
150 North Michigan, #2145	Chicago IL 60601	312-726-1120

Singapore
Singapore Promotion Board

8484 Wilshire Blvd, #510	Beverly Hills CA 90211	213-852-1901
333 N. Michigan Ave, #818	Chicago IL 60601	312-220-0099
590 5th Ave, 12th Floor	New York NY 10036	212-302-4861

Spain
Nat Tourist Office of Spain

845 North Michigan Ave	Chicago IL 60611	312-642-1992
8383 Wilshire Blvd	Beverly Hills CA 90211	213-658-7188
1221 Brickell Ave	Miami FL 33131	305-358-1992

Sri Lanka
Embassy of Sri Lanka

2148 Wyoming Ave NW	Washington DC 20008	202-483-4025

Sweden
Swedish Tourist Board

655 Third Ave	New York NY 10017	212-949-2333

Switzerland
Swiss Nat Tourist Office

608 Fifth Ave	New York NY 10020	212-757-5944
150 N. Michigan, #2930	Chicago IL 60601	312-630-5840
260 Stockton St	San Francisco CA 94108	415-362-2260
222 North Sepulveda Blvd , #1570	El Segundo CA 90245	213-335-5980

Tahiti
Tahiti Tourist Bureau

6151 West Century Blvd, #1024	Los Angeles CA 90045	213- 649-2884

Taiwan
Republic of China Tourism Bureau

166 Geary St, #1605	San Francisco CA 94108	415-989-8677
1 World Trade Ctr, #7953	New York NY 10048	212-466-0691
333 N. Michigan Ave, #2329	Chicago IL 60601	312-346-1037

Thailand
Thailand Tourist Office
3440 Wilshire Blvd, #1100	Los Angeles CA 90019	213-382-2353
303 W. Wacker Dr, # 400	Chicago IL 60601	312-819-3990

Tourism Authority of Thailand
5 World Trade Ctr, # 2449	New York NY 10048	212-432-0433

Tonga
Tonga Consulate General
360 Post St, #604	San Francisco CA 94108	415-781-0365

Trinidad/Tobago
Trinidad & Tobago Tourist Board
400 Madison Ave, # 712	New York NY 10017	212-838-7750

Turkey
Consulate Gen. of Turkish Republic
1221 Broadway, Plaza Level #13205	Auckland CA 94612	415-362-0912

Turkish Govt. Tourism & Info Office
821 United Nations Plaza	New York NY 10017	212-687-2194

Supplies to Bring

Office Supplies

Calculator / batteries

Clipboard with pen or pencil attached

Correction fluid

Envelope pen / pad for door

Laptop computer / printer

Marker pens

Note-size Post-its™

Paper clips

Pencils, pens

Personal address labels (for sending post cards)

Rubber bands

Scissors

Scotch tape™ / glue

Silver duct tape (suitcase repair)

Stapler / staples / staple remover

Typewriter / ribbons / batteries

White/colored paper, size A4 letter or international size

Company Supplies

Blank name tags

Brochures advertising other company cruises

Business cards

Extra tour operator luggage tags

Thank-you notes (for ship's staff) / invitations

Tour operator stationery / envelopes

Party Supplies

Balloons / balloon holders

Banners (birthday / anniversary / holiday)

Candles

Confetti

Curling ribbon / ribbon shredder

Door / table decorations

Greeting cards (Valentine's Day, birthday, anniversary, tent cards etc.)

Holiday decorations

Streamers

Miscellaneous Essentials

Passport (copy front page)
Airline tickets
Travelers checks
Name Badge
All tour documents
Umbrella

Appliances

Camera / batteries / film
Clock / batteries
AC - DC converters
Hair dryer (110 / 120V)
Steamer (most ships don't allow ironing in cabins)
Tape player and tapes

Cosmetics / Toiletries

(In addition to your normal toiletries and cosmetics)
Antiseptic ointment / lotion
Aspirin
Bandages
Cotton balls
Eye drops
Ginger pills for seasickness (or other seasick medication)
Moist towelettes
Q-tips
Sewing kit
Scissors
Sunburn / Sunscreen lotions

Major Officers and On-Board Staff

Captain: The master of the ship — in charge of everything. (Captains can no longer marry people at sea).

Staff Captain: Second in command.

Chief Engineer: In charge of the ship's engine room.

Hotel Manager: Responsible for cabin assignments on board, changes, upgrades and cabin problems; supervises all cabin stewards and schedules housekeeping staff.

Chief Purser: Responsible for the ship's purse, or money; office manager who oversees money, information, and paperwork on board and passenger safety deposit boxes; works with port authorities and customs in clearing the ship at each port.

Chief Radio Officer: In charge of ship-to-shore communications.

Cruise Director: Master of ceremonies on the ship; in charge of passenger entertainment and social staff; schedules cruise host briefings and sometimes cocktail parties.

Bar Manager: Responsible for quality control of drinks served in the lounges and staff scheduling; sometimes books group parties and activities.

Passenger Service Representative: Responsible for resolving on-board passenger problems, initial booking problems, ticketing for return flights and seating the plane.

Ship's Doctor: Responsible for medical services during the cruise.

Cabin Stewards: Responsible for the cleanliness of cabins, room service for cabin meals and snacks, and minor cabin problems.

Maitre d':   The overall authority in the dining room: assigns the tables, makes table changes and supervises waiters and busboys.

Dining Room Waiters: Wait on tables in the dining room and serve at midnight buffets as well as poolside buffets for breakfast, lunch, and dinner.

Busboys: Assist the waiters. Pour water, serve bread, bring silverware, help serve and clear tables.

Social Hostess: May introduce passengers to the captain on the captain's formal welcome and farewell nights; assists social staff at parties and other activities.

Ship's Male Cruise Hosts: These men are employed by the ship to dance with and provide company for single female passengers. Although the ship refers to them as "Cruise Hosts," they do not perform any of the functions of a professional cruise host described in this book.

Entertainers: Entertain passengers with stage shows and cabaret acts.

Shore Excursion Manager: Responsible for selling and coordinating shore excursion and sometimes, giving shore excursion talks; distributes tickets, makes decisions on exchanges and refunds, decides on free excursions for cruise hosts, orders coaches from ground operators, coordinates tour departures, and is on the pier to dispatch tours and coaches.

Casino Manager: Responsible for running the casino.

Youth Counselors: Ship's staff who provide entertainment, parties, and activities for children on board the ship.

Embarkation Day Check-Off List

Day One

1. *Find your cabin*
   - ☐ Read the ship's newspaper to see the events of the day.

2. *Familiarize yourself with the ship*

3. *Check in with the purser's office*
   - ☐ Confirm group's cabin numbers
   - ☐ Leave a copy of your passenger list
   - ☐ Ask about copying letters (if necessary)
   - ☐ Check on copying facilities and privileges

4. *Contact the cruise director*
   - ☐ Confirm times and dates of important ship activities (e.g., captain's welcome party, repeaters' party)
   - ☐ Arrange your cocktail party times and places
   - ☐ Arrange your briefing time and place
   - ☐ Arrange your office hours time and place

5. *Contact the bar manager*
   - ☐ Arrange cocktail party (if not done through the cruise director)

6. *Meet with the maitre d'*
   - ☐ Check your clients' table requests
   - ☐ Solve known seating problems
   - ☐ Provide a list of birthdays and anniversaries
   - ☐ Obtain a dining room seating chart

7. *Copy/deliver information*
   - ☐ Welcome letter
   - ☐ Passenger name list
   - ☐ Any other company information or port information

8. *Be back with the maitre d' at specified time for passengers to make dining room seating changes*

9. *Attend the lifeboat drill (if held on the first day)*

10. *Attend any port or shore excursion talks and/or ship's introductions*

11. *Attend dinner*

12. *Tape your envelope, note pad, and pen to your cabin door*

13. *Place decorations on clients' cabin doors*

Day Two

1. *Hold your initial briefing (if not done on the first day)*

2. *Give the ship's doctor a list of your passengers, and arrange for wheelchairs, if necessary*

3. *Set up a master charge account at the purser's office*

4. *Check with the shore excursion manager regarding a group buy (if not done the first day)*

Quiz Answers

Travel Quiz

1. Santa Fe, New Mexico (1609)
2. Bugs Bunny
3. $2.50 a day
   (or amount in cruise brochure)
4. Off Baja California
   in the Sea of Cortez
5. Jamaica
6. Del Mar
7. Switzerland
8. Istanbul
9. Copenhagen
10. Denmark
11. Maximum size for carry-ons
12. Between Nairobi and
    Mombassa, Kenya
13. Michelin
14. Jamaica
15. Helsinki
16. Yes, once
17. In the Australian state of
    New South Wales
18. Wine drinking
19. The Quebec Winter Carnival
20. The Lambada

Flags

1. United Kingdom
2. Yougoslavia
3. Norway
4. Swiss
5. Greece
6. Panama
7. Czechoslovakia
8. Australia
9. Canada
10. Chili
11. USA
12. Liberia
13. Israel
14. Turkey
15. Iraq
16. Pakistan
17. Jamaica
18. Japan
19. N. Korea

Country Currencies

1. K	5. Q	9. S	13. D	17. T
2. F	6. O	10. M	14. H	18. A
3. J	7. L	11. I	15. G	19. E
4. R	8. N	12. C	16. B	20. P

Party Supplies and Decorations

Some tour operators will provide a small budget for party items. Find decorations at party stores, toy stores, drug stores, and discount stores. Party stores often have a half-price section on discontinued items. For example, purchase Christmas decorations just prior to or after Christmas to use on next year's Christmas cruise.

Many companies also specialize in party items. One is the Oriental Trading Company in Omaha, Nebraska, phone (402) 331-5511. They have balloons, party hats, streamers, confetti, and lots of theme decorations. Call them for a free catalog. Orders are taken by phone and can be sent COD or billed to your credit card.

If there is a wholesale flower market in your city, they often have outlets open to the public that carry party supplies at discount prices.

Check in the yellow pages under Party (supplies/favors) for stores in your area.

Clothing

It is hard to include an exact clothing list. What you take will depend on the length of the cruise, the destination, climate and the quality of the cruise line. Here are some guidelines you can follow:

Plan on three outfits per day — one for shore excursions, one for the remainder of the day on the ship, and one for dinner. Some days you may require only two outfits.

Women should take two formal or semi-formal outfits and one theme-night outfit (also useful for masquerade night). (Use your cruise itinerary to mark the numbers of days you will be on board. Look through the information in your packet from the cruise line and look for all the events to be held on the ship — for example, a Greek night, Pastel night, or Western theme.) Port outfits will depend on the destination: you may want shorts, or rain slickers and boots, or a windbreaker. Again, you can count how many formal, semi-formal, and casual nights are listed for the cruise and pack an outfit for each evening. Don't forget that you can mix and match. Pack comfortable walking shoes, and jackets or a wrap for the evening. (Most ships are heavily air-conditioned.) Also, be sure to pack a bathing suit and warm-up suit for exercise activities.

Men will require a tuxedo or dark suit for formal and semi-formal nights. A sports coat and slacks will be appropriate for informal nights and slacks and sweater or shirt for casual nights.

Computer Programs
Used in This Manual

This manual and the documents used for illustration were produced on a Macintosh computer using various software programs. The following is a description of the computer programs used and the documents produced in each for purposes of this book:

PageMaker 4.2

Desktop publishing program by Aldus Corporation. 411 First Avenue South, Seattle, WA 98104, Telephone (206) 622-5500.

Documents Produced:

1. Certificates for International Sailor, First-Time Sailors, and Crossing the Equator
2. Group Dining Request Form
3. Confidential Client Information Sheet
4. Cruise Data Sheet*
5. Port Letters*
6. Quizzes*
7. Foreign Phrases*
8. Record of Purchases*
9. Briefing Notices*
10. Welcome Letter*
11. Office Hours Notice*
12. *Cruise Hosting* (this manual - not available on disk)

* These documents can also be produced in Word.

Word 5.0

Word processing program by Microsoft Corporation, 16011 NE 36th Way, Redmond, WA, Telephone (206) 882-8080.

See * items under PageMaker 4.2

FileMaker Pro

Database program by Claris Corporation, 5201 Patrick Henry Drive, Santa Clara, CA 95052, Telephone (408) 987-7000.

Documents Produced: Entire client database to create:

1. Pre- and Post-Tour List

2. Rooming List

3. Birthday and Anniversary List

4. Dining room seating information

5. Name and address information (for labels or envelopes)

6. Layouts for certificates (name, destination, dates)

7. Tourist Bureau List

Excel 4.0

Spreadsheet program by Microsoft Corporation, One Microsoft Way, Redmond, WA 98052, Telephone (206) 454-2030.

Documents Produced:

1. Currency Conversion Chart

MapArt

Presentation quality clip art maps by MicroMaps Software, 9 Church Street, P.O. Box 757, Lambertville, NJ 08530, Telephone (609) 397-1611.

Documents Produced:

1. Country map of South America

Cruise Hosting Program

Executive Enterprises is a computer consulting and programming company owned and operated by the author of this book. It is located at, Kappas Marina, East Pier #8, Sausalito, CA 94966, Telephone (415) 331-1808, FAX (415) 957-9474.

Providing you already own a Macintosh computer and the software programs discussed in this manual, a *Cruise Hosting Program Disk* is available. It includes a database program that enables you to enter all your tour information and easily create all the cruise host documents exhibited in this book. Depending on your computer hardware and software, this program can be customized to fit individual and agency needs. Documents and portions of programs can also be purchased separately on disk or hard copy.

Another service provided by Executive Enterprises is customizing computer programs for the general running of your agency. These include: costing and pricing programs for hotels, attractions, restaurants and transportation as well as programs to produce itineraries, contracts, invoices, vouchers and much more.

For more information, please complete the computer order form at the back of this book.

About International Tour Management Institute

International Tour Management Institute, Inc. was established in 1976. It is the first certified school in the United States designed specifically to train professional cruise hosts and tour directors/guides and to establish the understanding of the principles and ethics of tour management. Because emphasis is on practical field experience, more than half the program involves supervised training in the field.

The Institute conducts a total of five training classes a year in San Francisco, Los Angeles and Boston. Instructors are active travel professionals with 20+ years of experience in the travel industry. Classes are limited to 28 students. A full-time placement counselor works with more than 600 top tour companies in the United States to provide lifetime career counseling and placement assistance for all Institute graduates.

The school is a member of the National Tour Association, Better Business Bureau, American Society of Travel Agents, and the Convention and Visitors Bureaus of Boston and San Francisco.

For more information and a brochure, contact:

International Tour Management Institute, Inc. 625 Market Street, Suite 610, San Francisco, CA 94105, Telephone (415) 957-9489.

Index

Book Order Form

Please send:

_____ copies of *Cruise Hosting* at $19.95 USA ($24.95 Canada)
(California residents add 7.25% sales tax.)

SHIP TO

Name _____

Address _____

City _____ State _____ Zip _____

Phone _____ Fax _____

CALCULATIONS

Books	_____
Shipping	_____
7.25% Tax	_____
Total Due	_____

SHIPPING CHARGES

Mail — $2.00 for first book and 75¢ for each additional book

Federal Express — $10.00 per book

UPS — $3.50 per book

MAILING ADDRESS

Travel Time Publishing
P.O. Box 233, Sausalito, CA 94966 • (415) 331-1808

Book Order Form

Please send:

_____ copies of *Cruise Hosting* at $19.95 USA ($24.95 Canada)
(California residents add 7.25% sales tax.)

SHIP TO

Name _____

Address_____

City _____ State _____ Zip _____

Phone _____ Fax_____

CALCULATIONS

Books   _____

Shipping   _____

7.25% Tax   _____

Total Due _____

SHIPPING CHARGES

Mail $2.00 for first book
and 75¢ for each
additional book

Federal
Express $10.00 per book

UPS $3.50 per book

MAILING ADDRESS

Travel Time Publishing
P.O. Box 233, Sausalito, CA 94966 • (415) 331-1808

Custom Computer Programs

Name _____

Agency _____

Address _____

City _____ State _____ Zip _____

Phone _____ Fax _____

Macintosh Computer Model _____ Memory Size _____ Hard Drive Size _____

Printer Model _____

I own the following software:

Program	Version
Word	_____
Excel	_____
PageMaker	_____
FileMaker	_____
MapArt	_____

I am interested in information on the following:

_____ A Cruise Hosting Program modified for my needs

_____ A custom database for my agency including hotels, restaurants, attractions, transportation, tour booking, invoicing, itineraries, etc.

_____ Seminars or speaking engagements

_____ Individual documents (certificates and forms referenced in List of Examples) Circle numbers below:

2.4	2.5	3.1	3.2	3.3
3.4	3.5	3.6	3.8	3.10
4.3	4.7	4.8	4.9	4.10
4.11	4.12	4.13	4.14	4.15
4.16	12.1	14.1	14.2	14.3

Travel Time Publishing   P.O. Box 233, Sausalito, CA 94966 • (415) 331-1808

Custom Computer Programs

Name _____

Agency _____

Address _____

City _____ State _____ Zip _____

Phone _____ Fax _____

Macintosh Computer Model _____ Memory Size _____ Hard Drive Size _____

Printer Model _____

I own the following software:

Program	Version
Word	_____
Excel	_____
PageMaker	_____
FileMaker	_____
MapArt	_____

I am interested in information on the following:

____ A Cruise Hosting Program modified for my needs

____ A custom database for my agency including hotels, restaurants, attractions, transportation, tour booking, invoicing, itineraries, etc.

____ Seminars or speaking engagements

____ Individual documents (certificates and forms referenced in List of Examples) Circle numbers below:

2.4	2.5	3.1	3.2	3.3
3.4	3.5	3.6	3.8	3.10
4.3	4.7	4.8	4.9	4.10
4.11	4.12	4.13	4.14	4.15
4.16	12.1	14.1	14.2	14.3

Travel Time Publishing   P.O. Box 233, Sausalito, CA 94966 • (415) 331-1808